# The Computer
# CONSULTANT'S
# WORKBOOK

## JANET
## RUHL

TECHNION BOOKS

D1372430

Copyright © 1996 Janet Ruhl

All rights reserved.

Printed in the United States of America

Published by Technion Books
Ruhl Computer Services
P.O. Box 171
Leverett, MA  01054
Email: 71121.1065@compuserve.com

Additional copies of this book may be ordered from the publisher.
Please include $2.00 for postage and handling. For information about
volume discounts please contact the publisher at the above address.

Reproduction or translation of any part of this work beyond
that permitted by Section 107 or 108 of the 1976 United
States Copyright Act without the permission of the copyright
owner is unlawful. Requests for permission or further information
should be addressed to Permissions Department, Technion Books.

This publication is designed to provide accurate and authoritative
information in regard to the subject matter covered. It is sold with
the understanding that the publisher and author are not engaged in
rendering legal, accounting, or other professional services. If legal
advice or other expert assistance is required, the services of a
competent professional person should be sought. FROM A
DECLARATION OF PRINCIPLES JOINTLY ADOPTED BY A
COMMITTEE OF THE AMERICAN BAR ASSOCIATION AND
A COMMITTEE OF PUBLISHERS

LIBRARY OF CONGRESS CATALOG CARD NUMBER: 95-90495
ISBN NUMBER: 0-9647116-0-5

# ACKNOWLEDGMENTS

Thanks are due, as always, to the denizens of Compuserve's Computer Consultants Forum, who each day teach me new things about consulting. Thanks go too to the accomplished group of professionals who attended my "Getting Started in Consulting" seminar whose active participation and excellent questions have given me a much better idea of what new consultants need to know.

Special thanks go also to my "beta readers," Tom Scott and Steve Zilora, for wading through this manuscript as it made its way towards completion and for giving me the benefit of their own considerable experience in consulting. Thanks go also to Steve Wolfson for sharing with me his unique blend of technical and metaphysical assistance, and to Alaina Snipper for her expert contribution to the cover design. Thanks go too to Bruce Scofield for setting me such a fine example of successful niche publishing with his One Reed Publications. His down-to-earth, "it's no big deal" advice has had a lot to do with my getting up the courage to take this entrepreneurial plunge.

Finally, I must thank my two wonderful children who, with their usual good-humor, have tolerated my book-obsessed state and cheerfully eaten frozen pizza while I fussed with fonts. I don't know whether to celebrate or worry that nine-year-old David already scores high on the "Consultant's Personality Quiz" but I'm awfully glad that he got its jokes. And what can I say about my daughter Joanna? Back in 1988 I dedicated my first book to her when she had just learned how to read. Now at twelve she is a competent and capable *proofreader* whose grasp of the finer points of grammar and usage is a whole lot stronger than my own. No mother could ask for more!

# CONTENTS

## WORKSHEETS

## FACT SHEETS

## EXAMPLES

## TABLES

# INTRODUCTION

I f you dream of making a living as a computer consultant this book is for you. In its pages you'll find the information you need to make that dream a reality. With the advice and facts you will find here you will be able to:

- Determine if you have what it takes to succeed in consulting

- Set up your consulting practice

- Figure out how much to charge

- Find the clients you need

- Sell your services to those clients

- Protect yourself with contracts

- Handle common problems on the job

- Work with third party consulting firms

You'll also learn about the "gotchas" that lurk for the unwary, and share the tips and tricks experienced consultants know. You'll find help in crafting a customized marketing plan suited to the particular kind of consulting you practice. You'll find exercises to help you improve your ability to communicate with acquaintances, colleagues, and clients. You'll also find examples of effective business letters, phone scripts, resumes, proposals, and sales dialogues you can use as models for your own business communications.

## HOW IS THIS INFORMATION PRESENTED?

We know you're busy, and that you've already got a mountain of computer-related reading piling up on your desk. So our goal here is to give you the information you need in the fastest, most accessible way possible.

### STRIPPED DOWN FORMAT

This book is designed so you can read it quickly. There's lots of meat here, and some humor, but we've dispensed with everything but the material you really need to know.

### FACT SHEETS

Wherever possible, information you will need to refer to more than once has been split out into a Fact Sheet and the explanation of why these facts *are* facts has been put in a separate discussion section. This allows you to retrieve this information when you need it without having to plow through the accompanying explanations.

### COMPLETE EXAMPLES

There are lots of sample documents, scripts, and dialogues in the pages ahead. They highlight the principles you'll need to understand to create your own business materials, and make the most of the conversational opportunities you encounter.

### WORKSHEETS AND QUESTIONNAIRES

You'll also find a wealth of worksheets and questionnaires in these pages. These are not the space-filling fluff that pad out some how-to books, but exercises that have been tested by participants in my "Getting Started in Consulting" workshop. Every worksheet you'll find in this book features questions whose answers may well determine whether your consulting practice will succeed or fail.

### *SOAP BOXES*

Scattered throughout this book you'll also find pullout sections we've nicknamed "Soap Boxes." They're designed to help you improve your ability to speak in public, both to individual clients and to groups. Each Soap Box contains a single exercise geared to the chapter material. Early exercises prompt you to come up with answers to the questions prospects and clients are likely to ask you. More advanced Soap Box exercises help you prepare speeches you can use to promote your consulting work.

## SOAP BOX

To get the most out of these exercises, tape your presentation. Then listen to the playback several days later. Once you've become comfortable working with these tapes, try videotaping yourself as you speak.

If you're like most people, you'll feel like an idiot the first time you hear yourself declaim. But if you aren't willing to risk sounding like an idiot, you aren't likely to make it as a consultant.

## WHERE DOES THIS INFORMATION COME FROM?

The information you'll find summarized in this book has been distilled from eight years of daily participation on Compuserve's Computer Consultants Forum. Each year more than thirty thousand people from around the world come to this on-line bulletin board to discuss how to handle the issues that come up in their own consulting careers.

In my previous book, *The Computer Consultant's Guide: Real-Life Strategies For Building A Successful Consulting Career*, I provided readers with samples of the advice forum visitors had shared over the years. While *The Computer*

*Consultant's Workbook* covers many of the same topics discussed in the *Guide* it does it in an entirely new way. The focus in the earlier book was on the experiences and wisdom of successful—and sometimes not so successful—computer consultants. The focus here is on *you.*

The exercises and worksheets you'll find in this book are intended to get you thinking, planning, and, most of all, moving, in your own consulting career. The sample dialogues and documents you'll find in these pages answer the nuts and bolts "how do I do it?" questions there wasn't room to cover in the earlier book.

Finally, while the *Guide* spoke repeatedly about the importance of honing your listening and communication skills, this book goes a step further by giving you dozens of practical tips and exercises that will help you assess and improve those skills.

## HOW TO USE THIS BOOK

You may want to begin by reading this book through from cover to cover. Then, no matter how much consulting experience you may already have, take the time to work through the exercises you'll find in Chapter One, *Are You Ready for Consulting?* Not only will the answers you come up with be useful when you come to the exercises and worksheets you'll find in the rest of the book, but there is no consultant, no matter how experienced, who cannot benefit from rethinking the questions you'll find presented in this chapter.

Then keep this book handy. Review the "What You Have To Find Out at the First Interview" worksheet *before* you head out to meet with a potential client. Return to the "Proposal Worksheet" each time you prepare a proposal. When it's time to adjust your rate, use the rate worksheets to come up with an appropriate rate structure. Return to the discussion of how various marketing techniques work every now and then when it's time to renew your marketing efforts.

Finally, remember that every consulting practice changes over the years. Even if you're highly experienced, you can always learn something new from reviewing the questions you'll find in these worksheets and rethinking the way you're running your business.

# 1  ARE YOU READY
# FOR CONSULTING?

**CHAPTER OBJECTIVE**

**Determine if you've got what it takes to be a successful computer consultant**

- Learn about the different kinds of computer consulting
- Determine what niche you fit into and whether it is one that can support a consulting career
- Assess your consulting credentials
- Think through where you'll find your clients
- Explore whether you have the kind of personality that flourishes in consulting
- Make sure you won't get nailed by the hidden "gotchas" that preclude consulting

Could you make it as a consultant? The material in this chapter will help you make that decision. Would you enjoy a consulting career? You'll find that answer here too. But whether or not you're ready—or willing—to start consulting now, the material you'll find in these pages will show you how to prepare now for future consulting success.

# WHAT DO CONSULTANTS DO?

The term "computer consultant" covers a lot of territory, taking in nationally known experts as well as people who help install WordPerfect on a neighbor's machine. Here are capsule descriptions of the main subtypes of the species. Do any of them sound like you?

## TYPES OF CONSULTANTS

**The Genius:**  He has a pony tail, wears sneakers to the interview, and knows that he'll get the job because he's one of five people in the country who can do what he does and the other four are busy.

**The Maven:**  She's quoted in *Forbes* or *The Wall Street Journal*. She used to be a top executive of a major corporation, or she's the author of a well-known book or expensive industry newsletter. Nobody knows exactly what she does now, but she sure *looks* successful.

**The Entrepreneur:**  He's identified a niche in the local business community and made his name filling it. He's got ten employees and earns more money than he ever dreamed of, but it's been five years since he's taken a day off.

**The Cottage Industrialist:**  She works from home, by herself. Companies outsource work to her that in many cases they can no longer do in-house. She gets paid $2,000–10,000 for each project, but she has trouble remembering to get out of the house once every month or so.

**The Contractor:**  He quit his job, or got laid off. Now he works the same job for a high hourly rate. He gets no benefits, no insurance, and no job security. If he plays it right, he can earn $60K a year and take two months of vacation. If he plays it wrong he's going to end up on welfare. So he better know what he's doing.

**The Organization [Wo]man:**  Her employer puts "consultant" on her business cards and bills her out at $225/hr. Since she works 60 hours a week, it's too bad she only gets to keep eight cents of each of those luscious billing dollars.

**The Fuller Brush Man:**  He's peddling his services door-to-door to mom and pop businesses and home computer owners. He probably isn't going to earn enough for a pink Cadillac.

**The Moonlighter:**  She does work for friends and small businesses at night or on weekends. Someday she's going to get brave and quit that day job.

What are clients getting from all this? Why do so many clients use consultants? The reasons are not always the obvious ones, and anyone considering consulting as a career would do well to make themselves aware of the forces behind clients' growing use of consultants.

## WHY CLIENTS USE CONSULTANTS—The Reasons From Best to Worst

- Limited need for specialized technical services.

- Limited budget for technical services, no matter how much they are needed.

- Need for the fresh approaches and objectivity an outsider can provide.

- Need to get a "seal of approval" on major policy moves.

- Need to get access to "insider" information.

- People with needed skills are not available as employees.

- Headcount restrictions preclude hiring employees, but budget is available for "miscellaneous services."

- Desire to save money on employee benefits.

- Desire to avoid compliance with laws regulating employee hiring and treatment on the job.

- Desire to avoid paying taxes and social security payments for workers—and, occasionally, the desire to avoid paying anything at all.

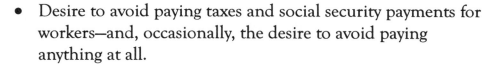

**GOTCHA!!**

One last reason clients hire a consultants is—

The need for a scapegoat.

Most successful consultants maintain that *Specialization* is the key to their success. Here are some of the areas of specialization that computer consultants have found success in.

## VIABLE NICHES

- Contract COBOL/DB2 programming for large corporate clients.

- Designing and supporting accounting applications written in Clipper.

- Writing ATM systems for banks.

- Providing computer system backup and recovery planning.

- Teaching classes about software, languages, or operating systems to a corporate audience.

- Designing and supporting industrial spray nozzle control software.

- Forensic consulting (testifying in court cases).

- Capacity planning and long-term strategic design.

- Training corporate staff in object oriented techniques and managing object oriented programming pilot projects.

- Network design, installation, and maintenance.

- Keeping custom software at financial institutions like banks and insurers up to date with the latest tax law changes.

- Implementing OCR (Optical Character Recognition) systems.

- Installing and supporting retail, medical, and legal systems.

- Firmware design for engineering applications.

- Compiler design.

- Gas and Oil Company applications.

- Software translation for foreign markets.

- Implementing computer-based adaptive devices for special needs populations in school systems.

## CONSULTING MYTHS AND REALITIES

**MYTH:** You should give free services to clients to boost lucrative hardware sales.

**REALITY:** Because of the fiercely competitive nature of the retail hardware business and the dominance of high volume superstores and mail order companies, successful computer consultants do just the opposite: they sell hardware at cost and make their money by providing support services.

**MYTH:** Home computer users represent a huge untapped market that will support a consulting business.

**REALITY:** Home computer users *need* help, but they rarely can afford to *pay* for it. The consultant who serves this niche must market constantly to find enough clients to keep working, and can usually only sell one or two hours of help to each client. Because so much time is wasted driving from client to client, it may be hard to find enough billable hours to keep profitable.

**MYTH:** It's easy to succeed if you provide service contracts for clients' existing hardware.

**REALITY:** Because of the dizzying pace at which hardware has evolved, it is almost impossible to keep enough parts in stock to support the hundreds of different configurations you will find at clients' offices. This makes it very hard to give clients the quick response they expect. If you *do* invest in a huge parts inventory, the parts you buy are likely to become obsolete while sitting on your shelves.

**MYTH:** Providing automated back-up services is a "can't fail" idea whose time has come.

**REALITY:** It's tough to convince clients they need this kind of service until they've lost some important data. So while this is a marketable service, you'll have to market long and hard to find enough clients to keep you in business—and you'll have lots of competition from other beginning consultants who have gotten the same bright idea.

## WORKSHEET: What's My Niche?

*Use this worksheet to determine whether the kind of consulting you're considering can support a long-term consulting career. You'll get the most out of it if you fill it in before you read the discussion that follows on Page 12.*

1. What is your area of expertise?

2. Are you a specialist or a generalist? If a specialist, what is your area of specialization?

3. How would you describe your services to a high level executive who is not familiar with the technical details of your niche?

4. Do you know anyone who makes a living as a consultant in this niche?

5. What is their background?  Is it at all like yours?

6. Will you need a lot of expensive retraining to keep up to date? Can you afford to pay for this training from what you expect to earn?

7. How dependent are you on a single vendor, product, industry, or technology?

8. If what you depend on were to vanish would you still be able to make a living?

9. After you have sold one service to a client, what follow-up services can you expect to sell the same client?

10. What would achieving consulting success mean to you?

## UNDERSTANDING YOUR ANSWERS TO THE "What's My Niche?" WORKSHEET

### COULD YOU DEFINE YOUR SPECIALTY SUCCINCTLY?

If you found it hard to describe what you do in any but the most generic terms, you've identified a problem. The more well defined your specialty is, the more easily you can describe it to others, and the more likely they will be to remember what you do and mention your work to others. This will make it a lot easier to market yourself. If you try to be all things to all people, you're more likely to end up selling nothing to nobody.

For example, if you tell friends, "I can do anything with computers" they're likely to nod politely and forget what you said. But if you describe yourself in a more targeted way, saying "I provide accounting software for retail stores," they're more likely to mention you when an acquaintance comments that she needs help upgrading her dress shop's computer system.

Since word of mouth is the number 1—and number 2 through 10—way that consultants get new clients, it's essential that you describe what you do in a way that ensures that people remember—and tell others—exactly what kind of consulting you do.

### HOW GOOD ARE YOU AT DESCRIBING WHAT YOU DO WHEN TALKING TO THE TECHNICALLY SIMPLE-MINDED?

Computer people often forget that not everyone speaks computerese—particularly the executives who have the fattest budgets for hiring consultants.

So, while you will need to use technical descriptions when talking with people who understand them, you must also be able to describe what you do in terms a nontechnical listener can understand.

For example, while it would be appropriate to tell the manager of a software development project, "I'm an experienced DB2 DBA," in casual conversation with ordinary people—and executives—you'd do better to say, "I design and improve the performance of large-scale mainframe-based financial databases."

### KNOWING FOLKS IN THE BUSINESS.

If you don't know anyone who makes a living as a consultant in the niche you plan to work in, it might be an opportunity—or it might just be a sign that the niche isn't viable.

This is particularly true if the niche you've identified is "training the home computer/small business user." This particular niche always appears underserved because it is impossible to make enough money at it to stay in business.

Then too, you'll find it much easier to *break into* consulting if you already know consultants who are hard at work in the niche you'd like to serve. That's because, far from being "the competition," other consultants in your niche are among your greatest resources. They are the people who can:

- Show you the ropes.
- Refer their overflow clients to you when they get busy.
- Bring you in as a subcontractor when they get a large project.
- Refer you to reputable brokers who can find you work.
- Prevent you from falling prey to known Clients From Hell, and Vampire Brokers.

But most of all, the existence of flourishing consultancies in your niche reassures you that the niche is viable.

### DO YOU HAVE THE SAME BACKGROUND AS THOSE WHO SUCCEED IN YOUR NICHE?

If you don't have a background similar to that of people who have already succeeded in the niche you'd like to enter, you better have a very good reason for thinking you can succeed in it. Because of how credential-driven consulting is, a mismatch between your credential and the credentials of those who succeed in a niche is usually a warning flag. If you're missing a credential that is common among successful consultants in a niche, at a minimum, you need to look into what it will take to acquire that credential.

An *oversupply* of credentials on your side may also flag a problem—or at least suggest that you need to do some investigating to make sure there isn't a good reason why people with your credential have avoided the niche. For example, there may be another niche that calls for that same credential and pays better.

## CAN YOU KEEP UP WITH THE TECHNOLOGY?

This is perhaps the most important—and most overlooked—question you can ask yourself before beginning a consulting career.

No matter what skills you start out with, in five years everything you know now will be obsolete. If you can't afford the training it will take to keep current—or if you don't see how you can get access to that training—then no matter how bright your prospects at the beginning of your consulting career, you will have trouble remaining viable.

This problem is particularly important for consultants who specialize in mainframe software or other specialties that flourish in the corporate world and require ongoing corporate-sponsored training.

## CAN YOU COPE WITH A CRUCIAL DEPENDENCY?

Why is dependency so important? Because the history of computer consulting shows that even the most solid-looking niches can disappear when business conditions change.

How many people do you know who are doing Wang word processor support right now? That was a hot niche in 1984. How do you think missile control specialists are doing now that the Cold War is over? Paradoxically, the very specialization that can make your consulting successful can also bring it to a screeching halt.

If your specialty makes you dependent on a single vendor, technology, or industry, keep up with its fortunes in the business press and make sure you get cross-training in some other specialty so that your business doesn't dry up if your main specialty goes under.

## CAN YOU PROVIDE FOLLOW-UP SERVICES?

Marketing is tough and most consultants hate doing it. It often takes as much work to find a client who will buy $250 worth of services as it does to find one who will buy $25,000 worth. That's why successful consultants almost always work with the kind of client who, if they satisfy them in the initial assignment, is likely to have a lot more work for them to do.

Your specialty should either be one for which clients have a bottomless thirst, such as contract programming in a corporate setting, or one where you will be able to offer clients a whole suite of related services once they've bought your initial offering. This kind of repeat business will let you put your time into doing paid work for a small but loyal clientele rather having to waste it on the continuous unpaid client hunting that is the fate of the consultant who offers a one-shot service.

With this in mind, you can also see why you are more likely to succeed in any niche if the type of client who is known to buy your services is used to spending $25,000 on consulting services each year, rather than $1,000.

## SOAP BOX

Based on your answers to the above questions, give a three minute talk describing the focus of your consulting practice to a nontechnical audience.

Questions your talk should answer include:

- What kind of work do you plan you do?
- What kind of client do you hope to serve?
- How strong is demand for this kind of service in your region?
- What is the long-term outlook for this kind of consulting?
- How would you like to see your business develop over the next five years? Ten years?

## WOULD CONSULTING SUCCESS MAKE YOU HAPPY?

Some successful consultants build up huge businesses that employ dozens of programmers and technicians. Others, by choice, work alone. Some fly all over the world serving a clientele of top decision makers. Others make a good living serving businesses in a single county. Some brag of earning hundreds of thousands of dollars. Others brag of taking three months off every year to play Rock and Roll.

Before you begin a consulting career, take the time to define what kind of success would satisfy *you*. Then make sure that the niche you're considering is one that allows for that kind of success. Use the following table to help yourself sanity check your choices

**Table 1. Niches and Lifestyle**

| Type Of Consultant | Lifestyle |
|---|---|
| **Contract Programmer** | Often a programming "temp" but may also provide higher level services. |
| | May work in a home office, by modem, or on-site 40 hours a week. |
| | Long periods "on the bench" between assignments are possible. They can be used for travel and hobbies—or for worrying about whether they'll ever land another assignment. |
| | Many contract programmers remain in business for 5 years or more. |
| **VARS/Reseller** | Sell, configure, install, and maintain hardware and software for businesses of all sizes working from a home office or storefront. |
| | May be on-call round the clock. Must keep up with dizzying technological and market changes. Must have excellent business and accounting skills and be able to deal with vendors. |
| | Must find backup if taking time off. May be in competition with mail order companies and large corporate "consulting" firms. May need to hire employees. |
| | Few remain in business more than 5 years. |

| Type Of Consultant | Lifestyle |
|---|---|
| **Custom Software Developer** | Develops "one of a kind" software to fit client needs. Rarely can this software be resold. Usually modifies a base system, either their own or a commercial product.<br><br>Profit centers include upgrades, training, and support contracts.<br><br>Requires excellent marketing skills and intimate knowledge of the client's way of doing business.<br><br>If system becomes a product can become wealthy, but this rarely happens.<br><br>Steady income possible but expect 80 hour weeks. Must find backup to support clients before taking time off. |
| **MIS Management Consultant** | Provide strategic planning, needs analysis, and outsourcing plans to high level MIS executives.<br><br>Publications and public speaking required.<br><br>Experience in MIS management useful. A network of solid contacts in MIS management required.<br><br>Very good income possible, but only to the few who achieve "expert" status.<br><br>Five year success common among experts, but experts are few. |
| **Industry Expert** | Previous high profile executive position in industry usually required. Books and columns in national media essential.<br><br>This role grows out of the management consultant role described above. |
| **Big Consulting Firm Consultant** | Employee of companies like Andersen Consulting or IBM. Works for modest salary. Sixty hour work weeks required. Work includes contract programming and promoting and implementing employers' turnkey systems.<br><br>Usually hired out of college or grad school with less than two years of work experience.<br><br>Most burn out in three years and are replaced by new college hires.<br><br>Not a good way to learn entrepreneurial consulting since big consulting firms do not operate like independent consultants. |

## DO YOU HAVE THE CREDENTIALS IT TAKES TO SUCCEED?

It's one thing to know how to get the job done. It's something else again to convince a stranger (a.k.a. potential client) that you have what it takes to do it. Choosing an effective area of specialization is not enough. You need to make sure that you have the credentials it takes to sell yourself in that niche.

But what does that mean? Most of us realize that we can't set up as a brain surgeon without an MD. But what constitutes a credential when it comes to the wild and woolly—and totally unregulated—field of computer consulting?

Traditional credentials include academic degrees, a history of holding top management jobs, professional certifications and awards. However, computer consultants often succeed without these traditional credentials—including degrees or certifications—as long as they are able to demonstrate that they've received equivalent training in the work place and can point to real-world achievements.

Here are a variety of real world credentials, along with examples of how you might communicate them to a client.

## TYPES OF CREDENTIALS

### YEARS OF EXPERIENCE CREDENTIAL:

**Example:** *"I've been designing accounting systems for small businesses for ten years. I got my training working as a senior analyst at Jones Accounting Systems and have been developing systems on my own as an independent consultant for the past four years."*

## YEARS OF EXPERIENCE CREDENTIAL ENHANCED WITH NAME BRAND EMPLOYER:

*Example:* "I spent twenty-two years designing telephone systems for businesses like yours as a Bell Systems and NYNEX engineer."

## ACHIEVEMENT CREDENTIAL:

*Example:* "I headed up the reengineering effort that replaced an aging reinsurance system at Colossal Insurance with an object oriented one that let the company cut headcount in half. Here's the Computerworld *article I wrote about that project."*

## NAME RECOGNITION CREDENTIAL:

*Example:* "I'm James Martin."

## EDUCATION CREDENTIAL:

*Example:* "I recently received a BSCS from MIT with a specialization in Artificial Intelligence applications."

## QUALITY CREDENTIAL:

*Example:* "Here is a list of clients who have had me install my Video Retailer software. Please feel free to contact any of these people and ask them about the quality of my work. If you'd like to see a demo of my package I'd be happy to arrange it."

## CERTIFICATIONS

Because there is no generally accepted credential for computer professionals corresponding to the accountant's CPA or the doctor's MD, a host of organizations, nonprofit and for profit, have sprung up to offer a bewildering array of certifications.

Nonprofit organizations issuing such certifications include The Institute for Certification of Computer Professionals (ICCP) which grants the CCP (Certified Computer Professional) and several other certifications and the EDP Auditors Association which offers the CISA (Certified Internal Systems Auditor) certification.

The best known vendor-supplied certifications are Novell's Certified Novell Engineer (CNE) and those offered by Microsoft's Microsoft Certified Systems Developer program.

Over the years, a host of for-profit schools have sprung up offering courses designed to help people pass the tests required to earn these vendor-supplied certifications. These courses can cost many thousands of dollars—above and beyond the hefty fees you'll pay to take the vendor-supplied certification exams.

Advertising for these courses often implies that once you have attained the vendor certification clients will follow automatically. In reality, what such certifications do for you—assuming the certification is one your clients recognize—is allow you to raise your rates if you've already established yourself as a consultant in the niche they relate to. However, a certification alone is not likely to bring you new clients and so should not be considered a shortcut to a consulting career.

# THE CERTIFICATION CONTROVERSY

The subject of how worthwhile various certifications might be is a controversial topic within the consulting community.

Those who argue FOR them maintain that:

- Certifications are an excellent way to distinguish yourself from other consultants.

- Certifications convince clients you know your stuff.

- Certifications help clients evaluate your level of expertise.

- Certifications requiring expensive, lengthy testing show that you're serious about being a professional in your field.

Those who argue AGAINST reply that:

- Most clients have never heard of certifications such as the CCP, so getting one can be an expensive, time-consuming ego-trip.

- Vendor certification programs like the CNE program are marketing ploys by vendors trying to make their product an industry standard, not a real proof of competence.

- Good test takers can pass certification tests without being able to do the work the certification relates to. Many people take certification tests in the hope of entering a field in which they have no real world experience, cheapening the value of the certification.

- The only time to take a certification seriously is if you start seeing it listed in RFPs.

## WORKSHEET: Evaluate Your Credentials

*Use the following questions to help yourself make the most of your credentials–both traditional and "real world" ones.*

1. List your three most important credentials or achievements in descending order.

2. If you are currently consulting, what is the primary reason that clients ask you back to do repeat work? If you are not yet consulting, what aspects of your work have received the most praise from others?

3. Ask some people who know you in a work capacity what they think are your greatest strengths. List them here.

4. How well do your strongest credentials relate to the specialty you've chosen?

5. What distinguishes you from others who provide the same kinds of service you provide?

6. Is there any weakness in your credentials?

7. When you present yourself to clients do you mention this weakness and excuse it, explain it, or otherwise try to compensate for it?

8. If you could "wave a magic wand" and get instant improvement, what change would you most like to make in your credentials or in the skills and services you have to offer clients?

**SOAP BOX**

Reply to the question,

### *"What's Your Background?"*

Keep your reply under two minutes in length. Concentrate on getting across your two or three most convincing credentials.

## UNDERSTANDING THE "Evaluate Your Credentials" WORKSHEET

### CREDENTIALS? I DON'T HAVE ANY CREDENTIALS!

Do your achievements and credentials sound wimpy even to you? Well, maybe you're a loser—or maybe you're just too humble.

Distinguishing between the two is not easy. That's why feedback from other people is so important. Because of the social conditioning that prevails in our society, women will often underestimate their abilities and achievements while men will overstate theirs. Feedback from others can help you get a more objective sense of whether you have real credentials.

If you can't come up with a traditional credential but do have real-world experience using computers in the workplace ask yourself:

- What systems have you designed, coded, modified, improved, or installed in the past year?

- Have you saved anyone a significant chunk of change by showing them how to use computers more effectively?

- Have you recently saved someone from disaster using some technical information you knew and they didn't?

If you have done any of the above, you've just found a credential. If you haven't, you better accept you aren't ready to start consulting. Consulting presumes expertise, and expertise derives from a long series of achievements.

If you don't have those kinds of achievements now, your first order of business must be to get them. Look at yourself as a "consultant in training" and do whatever it takes—including working for free as a volunteer for public service groups—to put something on your resume that will convince strangers that it will be worthwhile to pay you to do work for them.

Discovering that you don't have strong enough credentials to consider consulting now does not mean that you can't ever be a consultant. But it should get you thinking about what kind of experience you need to gain to be ready to consult in the future. And if you discover that you don't have what it takes to begin now, don't feel too bad. It's good that you have a realistic perception of where you fit in on the skill continuum. The people who end as "Consultants from Hell" are those who don't know their limits and take on work they don't have the experience and skills to pull off.

### EDUCATION AS YOUR MAIN CREDENTIAL

When presenting your credentials, have you highlighted your education? This can be a mistake. If you've just graduated from college or an MBA program, and have not worked in your field for some years as an employee, be prepared for a disillusioning shock when you flourish that degree in front of potential clients. Overwhelming respect is *not* likely to be their first reaction. "Oh, no! Another fresh-out-of-college know-it-all!" is.

The computer field has long been one in which seat-of-the-pants achievements have been valued above academic training. It is not coincidental that many of the world's most famous programmers and computer company founders were college drop outs.

Students who go from college into software development jobs—even impressive ones—quickly learn that it's best to shut up about their fancy degrees and let their work speak for itself. They also are likely to learn that the way business software and hardware work in real life bears little resemblance to the ideal scenarios presented by their professors—many of whom have never dealt with a real production system in their lives.

So if a degree is your only credential, the worst thing you could do right now is set up as a "consultant." Quality clients are not going to hire a new grad as a consultant, and those who *will* give you the job title of "consultant" straight out of college are almost always looking for cheap labor.

If you are about to graduate and want to be a real consultant in the future, your best bet is it to find a salaried job with a well-respected employer that will give you real-world experience and training in a technology that supports consulting careers. In a few years, when you've gotten past the usual beginners' mistakes and learned how things work, you'll be in an ideal situation to consult.

## TOO MANY CREDENTIALS

In most networking situations you only get 30 seconds to get your point across. If you submit a resume as long as your arm, no one will read more that a few paragraphs. So if you are lucky enough to have a hefty load of credentials, you need to focus on the few that are the strongest and most persuasive and get them across. Concentrate on those that are most closely related to the work you expect to do for clients, and those which they are most likely to recognize and respect.

## DOES YOUR CREDENTIAL FIT IN WITH YOUR SPECIALTY

This is probably the most important question you can ask yourself while evaluating your credentials. A degree in structural engineering may sound like a great credential—but not if you've decided to sell computer systems to lawyers.

Specialization is the key to consulting success, so you are not likely to find clients in your specialty unless you have at least one strong credential that trumpets "I'm an expert in this niche."

At a minimum you need to be able to point to having completed sophisticated projects in your area of expertise. It also helps to have raised your profile by speaking or writing publicly in your area of specialization. Equally useful is a "name brand" experience credential—like participation in a pilot program implementing some cutting edge technology at a well-known company.

You also should be able to direct clients to solid references who can vouch for your expertise. If you don't have a name brand or name recognition credential, it would help greatly if these references do. Clients are going to be a lot more impressed by a recommendation from a project manager at a Fortune 500 company, than they will by one from Manny the local dry cleaner—unless, of course, they're in the dry cleaning business themselves and your nifty new Windows-based dry cleaning package has just saved Manny a bunch of money.

## WHAT IMPRESSES YOU ISN'T NECESSARILY WHAT IMPRESSES CLIENTS

What past bosses have praised and rewarded you for is your best guide to what future clients will find most impressive. Often this is not what *you* consider most important.

For example, you may pride yourself on writing fast elegant subroutines, while your boss cares only that you always make your deadlines with code that works. You may consider your greatest achievement keeping your department's system from crashing for a year, while the boss may have rewarded you for some rinky-dink routine you wrote that printed the company logo on promotional T-shirts.

But your clients are going to be a lot like your past bosses—including the "dumbest" ones. So what impressed those bosses of yours may very well be what you have to trot out to land yourself those clients.

## DISTINGUISHING YOURSELF FROM THE COMPETITION

This might not sound like a "credential" item, but it is. If no one else in your town has a CNE certificate, that CNE of yours may be your most valuable credential. But if everyone has one (as is quickly becoming the case in many regions) and you and another CNE are bidding on a network installation job, the fact that you've installed 24 networks to his two is going to be a much stronger credential than the certification. So concentrate on identifying the things that make you more attractive than the competition in your niche, so that when it's time to spread those tail feathers and strut your stuff, you remember to get them across.

## DEALING WITH PERCEIVED WEAKNESSES

It's astonishing how many would-be consultants put their *worst* foot forward. Take the guy who introduces himself to you with the information that he recently got fired—or the woman whose only topic of conversation is the clients who complain about her work. Would-be consultants with otherwise stellar credentials have even been known to list layoffs and "personality conflicts with superiors" on printed resumes!

Perhaps these blunders stem from a longing to get the worst out of the way first or a misguided devotion to honesty. But mentioning negatives about yourself in a situation where a credential is called for is a great way to end your consulting career before it begins.

There is a time for being candid about career failures. But it comes long after you introduce yourself. Have explanations ready to deal with any significant problems that might be revealed when your history is explored but don't introduce them into the conversation yourself unless you have to.

For example, if you have been the victim of a downsizing and are asked "How come you left a great company like Megacorp?" an appropriate reply might be, "I left when management decided to eliminate our widget honing division as a cost cutting measure. Though I learned an enormous amount in my years at Megacorp, I'm really grateful that the downsizing gave me the push I needed to go out and put that knowledge to work for a broader range of clients." Then, as quickly as possible, return the discussion to the client's needs and what you can to do fill them.

## WHAT ABOUT OBVIOUS DISABILITIES?

The situation may be different if you have overcome a visible disability or some other circumstance that clients can't help but notice at a first meeting. In this case you may have to deal with the disability head on.

For example, if you are an eighteen-year-old who is still having trouble growing a beard competing for an important subcontract against a 40-year old Big Six partner, you probably will have to explicitly address the issue of your age. But the way to do it is *not* to say, "You probably think I can't do this job because I'm just a kid." Instead, say, "I'm young, but I've been doing paid programming work since I was thirteen" and then point to your list of satisfied corporate clients. Or invite the client to see a demo of one of your systems installed at the impressively furnished offices of a satisfied previous client.

Likewise, if you have a physical disability or are not a native English speaker, and worry that this may discourage potential clients—particularly since civil rights employment law may not apply in consulting situations—concentrate on getting your professional achievements across. You want to demonstrate that you've overcome whatever hurdles you've had to face. If possible, avoid having the conversation center on your disability and how you've overcome it as if *that* were your credential, and keep returning to discussions of your actual professional achievements.

### *WAVING THE MAGIC WAND*

Have you listed anything here? You have? Is it something that would improve your appeal to clients? Great! What are you waiting for? Figure out what it will take to add these "wish I hads" to your list of credentials and do whatever it takes to go after them!

## WHERE WILL YOU FIND YOUR CLIENTS?

Up until now we've been concentrating on you: your skills, your credentials, your personality. Now we get to the hard part—finding clients.

If you had to, you could probably be a consultant with poor skills, and weak credentials. You could maintain a practice of some sort with few business skills and a rotten personality. But you can't consult without clients.

Do you have a client already lined up? If so, good for you! You're reading this book at a time when it will do you the most good.

But don't make the mistake of thinking that having found one client means that you've made it. Like a mathematician proving a theorem, you must prove that your consulting works for "client n" and for "client n+1." In short, you need to know where your second and third and fourth clients are coming from before you assume you've got the client flow problem licked.

And if you don't have a client yet, what then?

Then it's time to start doing some serious thinking about where you're going to find the clients you need. You've done half of the work already, by defining your niche and ensuring that you have the credentials it takes to survive in that niche. Now it's time to take that analysis further, and answer the questions on the following worksheet.

## WORKSHEET: Who Is Your Client?

1. Describe your target client. Include industry, annual sales, geographical region, department that would hire you, and the level at which hiring decision are made.

2. Have any clients fitting this profile ever offered to pay you for performing the kind of service you intend to sell? You may include employee situations.

3. Does this type of client currently buy consulting services?

4. What dollar amount of your type of service does a typical client buy per year?

5. Does this client have employees who provide the same services you do? If so, why would they hire you?

6. Where can you meet this type of client? List specific user groups, professional meetings, and conferences.

7. What is the job title of the person you would approach at this type of client when marketing your services?

8. Does this type of client hire consultants from brokers or other third party providers? If so, do you know the names of reputable brokers in your region? Do you know if they'd be interested in placing you?

9. Does this client deal with retailers or other vendors who might be a good source of referrals to you? Do you know how to approach these retailers or vendors to ask them to refer you?

10. Do you know anyone currently working as a consultant who might be able to refer clients to you or offer you subcontract work?

---

## SOAP BOX

### *"My Client"*

Briefly describe your relationship with your target client to an imaginary bank officer who is evaluating your business for a loan. Be as detailed and persuasive as possible.

---

## UNDERSTANDING THE "WHO IS YOUR CLIENT" WORKSHEET

This worksheet is hard, and it's very likely that you've come up with several questions you were not able to answer. This doesn't mean your situation is hopeless, only that you have some work to do before you'll be able to market yourself effectively.

You should be able to find answers to the questions you can't answer now through networking with other consultants or interviewing business people in your industry. Once you know where to find the clients who buy the types of services you want to sell, you can then begin connecting up with them using the marketing techniques we'll be examining in Chapter Four, *How to Find Clients*.

### *WHEN YOU ARE VAGUE ABOUT YOUR CLIENT*

If you answered, "I don't know," to the majority of the questions above it may be a sign that you need to go back and do some more thinking about the specialty you were planning to concentrate on and the kinds of services you were planning to sell. If that is the case, ask yourself the following questions:

- *Have You Chosen A Specialty In Which You Have Little Experience?* If you have real experience working in a given area you should know something about the people who hire people with your kinds of skills. You should also know what kinds of people in the organizations you'd like to work for have the authority to hire consultants. Finally, you should also be aware of the kinds of business events they are likely to attend. If you don't know these things, you may not have as much real-world experience as you think you have.

- **When Choosing a Specialty, Did You Make Assumptions About Clients Based On Guesswork?** Working around computers can make us too logical. Just because clients *ought* to be out there buying a certain kind of service doesn't mean they are really buying it. You will need to talk to working consultants and other business people to uncover the facts about the clients who support the kind of consulting you want to do.

- **Are You Too Shy To Make The Phone Calls It Takes To Get The Answers You Need?** If so, get over it or give up the idea of consulting! Consultants have to be able to plunge in and ferret out facts, even if it means occasionally making pests of themselves. Call up old bosses, people you used to work with, and anyone else you know who might be able to give you the information you need, or at least point you to others who might have it.

## WHEN YOU CAN'T FIND A CLIENT

If you *still* can't get a handle on where you're going to find your clients, take it as a sign that you have some more work to do before you can become a consultant.

The consultants who last in this business usually start out with clients or consulting firms begging them to take on paid work. So if finding that first client is not a straightforward process, it's likely that you are *not* ready for consulting—even if lots of people are eager to have you do work for them for free.

If that is your situation, there is no need for despair. You can start working now on the strategies that will eventually get paying clients calling. Much of the advice you'll find in the rest of this book will show you just how to do that. But if it isn't happening now, *don't quit that day job.*

## DO YOU HAVE A CONSULTING PERSONALITY?

By now we've established that there are three things you need to have in order to succeed in consulting: a well-chosen niche, a compelling credential, and a very good idea of where to find your clients. But there is another set of issues you will want to consider before making a final decision about whether consulting is for you.

Expertise, credentials, and a client stream will let you succeed at consulting. But if you hate selling, loathe uproar, and have trouble keeping your bills under control, consulting "success" may feel like an endless nightmare.

Consulting is stressful. Moreover, it requires a slightly different mix of skills and a very different outlook than the salaried jobs that call for the same technical expertise. So a consulting career with its unique stresses is a lot easier to manage if you have a certain type of personality. There are even those who argue that if you have the classic "consulting personality" you are more likely to succeed—even with marginal technical skills and credentials—than someone with better skills who doesn't.

Use the light-hearted quiz you'll find on the next page to see how your personality stacks up against the classic consultant's personality profile.

## QUIZ: Do You Have a Consultant's Personality?

*The following quiz can help you decide if yours is a typical consultant's personality. You'll find a discussion of how to interpret your replies on Page 38.*

1.  For how long have you been getting paid for using the technical skills you plan to use in your consulting?
    a.   I've never been paid for this kind of work before
    b.   One year or less
    c.   Two to five years
    d.   More than five years
    e.   I've never been paid to use computers, but I've been a professional in my field for 20 years

2.  How many different jobs have you held over the past ten years?
    a.   One
    b.   Two
    c.   Five or less
    d.   I can't count that high—but my salary went up each time I switched jobs!

3.  At work are you considered
    a.   A dim bulb
    b.   A hardworking team player
    c.   A star performer—but perhaps a bit of a prima donna
    d.   A wizard

4.  Which of the following awards most excites you?
    a.   A gold plaque with your name inscribed as "employee of the month"
    b.   A raise
    c.   A promotion to management
    d.   A trip to Hawaii in February
    e.   A trip to Des Moines in February—to a week-long hands-on seminar on a hot new technology

5. How comfortable are you with writing?
   a. I hate writing!
   b. I can do the occasional report but that's about it
   c. I write too much—email is killing all my free time!
   d. I enjoy putting my ideas down on paper
   e. I've published three articles this year

6. How much business related reading do you do?
   a. Only what my boss makes me read
   b. A couple of trade magazines
   c. A few books a year and dozens of trade mags
   d. I read everything—even toilet paper wrappers

7. How comfortable are you with public speaking?
   a. Aaaaaaargh!
   b. Do I have to?
   c. Well, okay, maybe a few words—but don't tape it!
   d. I've just joined Toastmasters, I hope it helps
   e. What would you like me to talk about? Here's a list of the topics I have prepared

8. What's your favorite part of a new job?
   a. The interview—I love to show off
   b. The first few weeks—I love having a whole new world to explore
   c. After I've gotten my bearings, settled in, and made some friends
   d. After I've been around long enough to know everything and everyone—I don't like surprises

9. How much money do you have saved up for a rainy day?
   a. Did you have to ask? Anyway, I MIGHT win the lottery
   b. I could probably get through a month or two okay, but I'd have to check
   c. I have enough to get through six months without work if I had to

10. How well do you manage your money?
    a. There's usually some month left at the end of my money
    b. I drew up a budget last year as part of a New Years resolution but I lost it somewhere
    c. I don't know, I just give my paycheck to my spouse and they handle all that stuff
    d. Hold on, let me show you my nifty financial software package. See, I've earned $.0027 in interest while I've been filling out this questionnaire

11. How tolerant is your spouse of financial insecurity?
    a. Not very—We have a lot of expenses
    b. They make enough on their own job that it shouldn't matter what I make. Plus I'll use their benefits
    c. They want me to be happy with my work—whatever it takes
    d. I really don't know. I haven't discussed consulting with them yet
    e. I'm single

12. How much of your time does your family require?
    a. I figure consulting will be a great way to stay at home while my the kids are babies
    b. My spouse gets very burned up if I don't get home to dinner with the kids every night
    c. Nothing could be worse for our family than my day job. I haven't been home for a single scout meeting, baseball game, or school play in four years!
    d. My spouse is the best asset my consulting work could have—we'll spend more time together as they'll be working with me
    e. I'm single

## SCORING THE CONSULTANT'S PERSONALITY QUIZ

1.  Give yourself five points for each of the following answers:

    1d, 2c, 2d, 3c, 3d, 4b, 4e, 5c, 5e, 6c, 6d, 7e, 8a, 8b, 9c, 10d, 11b, 11e,12d, 12e.

2.  Give yourself three points for each of the following answers:

    1c, 2b, 5d, 6b, 7a, 7d, 9b, 11c, 12a, 12c

3.  Give yourself two points for each of the following answers:

    1e, 2b, 3b, 4c, 7c, 8c, 10c, 12a

## INTERPRETING YOUR SCORE:

**45–90:**          You sound like a consultant.

**15–44:**          Maybe, but read the next section before making any snap decisions.

**Less than 15:**          Don't quit your day job!

# UNDERSTANDING THE CONSULTANT'S PERSONALITY QUIZ

Here is a list of the personality characteristics that typify successful computer consultants:

## *Successful Consultants—*

- Develop their technical skills over a period of three to five years before they begin consulting.

- Have held a variety of jobs before consulting, rather than holding one long-term position.

- Are perceived by others as star performers.

- Are motivated by internal rewards. They prefer the thrill of problem solving to getting plaques and recognition.

- Devote enormous amounts of time to reading and studying in their field of concentration, even when not getting paid for it.

- Write and speak well.

- Enjoy meeting strangers.

- Enjoy what others consider stressful situations.

- Enjoy interviewing for new jobs.

- Enjoy the first weeks on a job more than the rest of the job.

- Enjoy learning new things.

- Manage money well and are able to budget.

- Have supportive families, spouses with their own incomes, or no family responsibilities.

- Have a good sense of their personal strengths and weaknesses. Know when to delegate. Know when to ask for help.

Why most of these characteristics would be an asset to the consultant should be obvious. But let's talk about the ones that might not be.

## EXCELLENT READING, WRITING AND SPEAKING SKILLS

These facilitate consulting success because so much of a consultant's job revolves around communicating with clients. You will have to write business letters, proposals, specifications, reports, summaries, and maybe even articles and books about your area of expertise. And with the growing use of electronic communications, your email style is becoming an increasingly important part of your overall business image.

## FAMILY SUPPORT

The wholehearted support of other family members is more important to attaining consulting success than many would-be consultants imagine. Like all entrepreneurs, consultants assume a higher level of risk in return for greater control over their professional destiny and potentially higher profits.

But while risk may sound appealing when touted by motivational speakers, in daily life it maps down to not knowing how much income you'll earn this year, or where you'll be working, or even *if* you'll be working. It means not being able to schedule vacations in advance because you don't know when you'll be busy and having to answer a phone that rings all night long because that's what it takes to keep your clients happy. It may also mean never being home for dinner and missing your children's class plays and even their graduations.

You may be able to handle the stresses that consulting would introduce into your life. You may even argue that you are already dealing with them since your supposedly "secure" job provides the same stresses without offering you consulting's control of your fate and its greater monetary rewards—and to some extent this may be true.

But though *you* may flourish in the atmosphere of uncertainty consulting entails, your spouse—who will *also* have to handle these stresses—may not. If your spouse or the rest of your family is unhappy, then no matter how well your consulting practice is going—the stress they introduce into your life may be enough to dynamite your career. That's why it's important to discuss what consulting will mean for your whole family with that family before you make any irrevocable decisions.

Many consultants have found that the ideal situation in which to begin consulting is when the spouse has a good job that provides family health insurance and other benefits as well as enough income to tide the family over the inevitable dry periods that occur during the consultant's start-up years—or, at the opposite extreme, when they have no family responsibilities at all.

## FAMILY RESPONSIBILITIES

Many people turn to consulting in hopes of improving the balance between family and work in their lives, but the occupational hazard of consulting is workaholism. Consultants find it easy to get sucked into working 80 and 100 hour weeks year in and year out. Yes, the money is piling up, but if you lose contact with your family because you're working all the time, is it worth it? Don't underestimate the amount of conflict that can be introduced into your marriage if once you become your own boss, the boss turns out to be a slave driver.

Nor is consulting necessarily the solution to a working mother's prayers. While consulting *can* be an excellent way to keep professional skills alive while stayong at home with young children, it is not realistic to expect to find and satisfy new clients with babies howling and toddlers underfoot. You'll still have to find reliable day care if you're to do any serious amount of consulting work, though the number of hours you will need to be away from the home can be cut back.

You are also more likely to be able to combine consulting and motherhood if you line up your clients and establish your consulting practice before the babies come. When you're wandering around in a state of intense sleep-deprivation, covered with baby puke, it is difficult to summon up what it takes to impress strangers with your expertise and professional competence. But though it is tough, it is not impossible, and plenty of women have done it—including myself.

## FINANCIAL RESOURCES

You don't need to have a lot of money to begin a consulting career, but you do need to have enough in the bank to tide you over the inevitable dry periods. Clients are notoriously slow to pay and there are always going to be contracts that fall through unexpectedly. So you need to be good at managing the money that you have.

Also, because the money you earn at consulting is more complicated to manage than the money you get at a salaried job, it is essential that you have at least a rudimentary grasp of accounting basics.

You will have to keep businesslike records for your taxes—and you'll have to remember that the checks clients write you merely represent your gross. After taxes and expenses your actual profit is going to be much less than the amounts on those client checks. So if you treat those checks the way you treated your old paychecks, and spend every cent of them when they come in, a few "fat" consulting checks could end up getting you into debt—or into trouble with the IRS.

## Table 2. Money Needed to Begin Consulting—By Niche

| Niche | Financial Resources Needed |
|---|---|
| Contract Programmer | Six months of living expenses. |
| VAR/Reseller | $5-10,000 to purchase equipment for resale. |
| | A good personal credit record to establish credit with wholesalers. |
| Custom Software Developer | Six months to one year of living expenses. |
| | Money to buy all upgrades to all standard software your custom software depends on. |
| Management Consultant | Six months to one year of living expenses. |
| | Money for travel and expenses of attending conventions, trade shows, etc. |
| Salaried Consulting Firm Employee | Enough to buy a very classy interview outfit. |

## WHAT YOU VALUE

Finally, to know whether you are going to be able to stick with consulting, you must be honest about what it is that you really want out of life.

If the admiration of your peers *is* what you most enjoy, you are going to hate consulting. The consultant comes in like the proverbial thief in the night, does his job, gets paid—if he's lucky—and disappears. There is little camaraderie with people you meet on the job and very little public recognition for even your most remarkable achievements. For those big bucks you're getting paid the client *expects* you to walk on water!

And if you hate stress and uproar, don't kid yourself that you are cut out for consulting. Consultants are almost always called in when things have reached a crisis, when everything is falling apart, and when the pain level has gotten high enough to justify spending big bucks on a solution. If you like a calm, placid life where all flows smoothly and things work the way they are supposed to, at least most of the time, you are going to hate consulting.

The people who flourish as consultants are those who derive their primary pleasure in life from learning new things and solving new problems—the kinds of people who plunge in and solve problems for free just for the fun of it because that's what they love to do. They are happy working on their own and don't care all that much what others may think of them, though they have enough political intelligence to work well alongside of others.

And while they may earn incomes of anywhere from $30,000 to $120,000 a year, money is not most successful consultants' primary motivator. Indeed, the consensus seems to be that it's not the money, but the freedom to work at what they love, doing things the way they want to do them, that makes consulting worthwhile to most consultants who stay in the business. They may appreciate the money, of course, but most would probably keep on working at exactly what they're working at now, even if they won the lottery.

## ARE YOU A TECHNOJUNKIE?

There's one last personality issue we need to consider before we leave this topic: Many people who are attracted to computer consulting are attracted to it because they are technojunkies—people whom others may consider to be addicted to computers and technology. Technojunkies are attracted to consulting because they see it as a way of earning a living doing what they love. The independence of consulting often appeals to them too, since their internal focus on things rather than people may cause them more than the usual amount of trouble when dealing with bosses and coworkers in salaried positions.

Many technojunkies do very well in consulting, but only after they recognize that their own intense love of technology is not shared by most of the people who are going to be paying them money. To succeed, they will have to invest as much effort into figuring out how clients' minds work and what clients themselves value as they do into understanding hardware and software.

Technojunkies with serious hardware habits also have to be aware that consultants are bombarded with "special offers" and opportunities to buy hardware and software. If—as many do—they spend more money on the techno-baubles they are exposed to than they earn from their practice, they may eventually be forced to face the fact that they aren't really in business, they're merely pursuing an expensive and time consuming hobby.

## HOW TO TELL IF YOU ARE A TECHNOJUNKIE

1. Do people laugh when you tell them you read **Computer Shopper** for the articles?

2. Do you have the latest release of every software package installed on your computer?

3. Does your current computer setup cost as much as you paid for your first house?

4. Have you networked your spouse's and children's computers?

5. Does your pet whine when it sees you reach for the keyboard?

6. Do you keep all your recipes stored in a relational database?

7. Do you secretly want to be a consultant because it will be an excuse to buy even more hardware and software?

If the answers to most of the above questions are "Yes," you are a technojunkie.

## WHEN CONSULTING MAY BE A BIG MISTAKE

Even if you've got skills, credentials, and a personality suited to consulting, there are still two circumstances in which consulting may prove to be an extremely bad idea. Unfortunately, many consultants don't discover these hidden "gotchas" until they've already quit their day jobs.

### UGLY GOTCHA #1 Consulting Makes It Tough—If Not Impossible—To Get Credit For Three Years.

Banks and other lenders will almost never lend to a self-employed person until they can show three years of tax returns from their business, each of them showing enough income to qualify for the loan.

If you've just started a business, it may not matter if you have signed contracts for work that will earn you $500,000 over the next year or even if your credit history is perfect. The bank may still turn you down, because the day you change your tax status from employee to independent contractor you've just started that three-years-no-credit clock ticking.

> **Note—**
>
> This "gotcha" does not apply to consultants who are forced to work as W-2 employees. (A subject discussed in Chapters Two and Five.)
>
> In fact, as a W-2 employee consultant you may even qualify for credit when you are "between assignments"— i.e., Unemployed.

So if you are planning to buy a house or car in the near future and cannot qualify for it on your spouse's income alone, put off consulting until the papers are signed.

### UGLY GOTCHA #2: It May Be Impossible To Get Health Insurance Coverage If You Or Any Member Of Your Family Has A Pre-Existing Condition

Here are just a few of the conditions that consultants have found disqualify them for all but the sleaziest of insurance plans:

- Asthma.
- Diabetes
- Heart surgery of any kind, ever

- Cancer surgery of any kind, ever
- Pregnancy
- Participation in marriage counseling sessions

In some cases consultants whose medical records reveal these pre-existing conditions cannot buy individual or group policies at all. In others they can—but at exorbitant prices. In yet others, the only policies they may find are ones that exclude all coverage for the named condition.

Even if you can qualify for health insurance, if you're used a premium employee benefit health insurance plan you may find the policies available to the self-employed nowhere near as comprehensive or as dependable as what you are used to. For example, some cheap policies aggressively marketed to the self-employed are written with weasel wording that makes it almost impossible to meet their deductibles. They calculate the deductible on a "per illness" basis rather than the usual annual claims basis and reset the deductible to zero any time you seek treatment for a new condition.

But even having a standard policy issued by a reputable insurer does not guarantee that you'll get your claims paid. Increasing numbers of insurers are keeping costs low by rejecting legitimate claims and making policy holders fight for their money.

A federal law (COBRA) ensures that if you leave a salaried job that provides health insurance benefits—whether because you were terminated or quit—you must be offered the chance to continue on in the employer's insurance plan for eighteen months after you leave your job. This is a "safety net" should you not be able to qualify for insurance on your own. But don't count on taking advantage of it until you've priced the premiums. Many corporate COBRA continuation health plans cost anywhere from $8,000 to $11,000 a year for family coverage and you will have to pay the entire premium yourself.

So obviously, if there's anything at all questionable in your family health history it's worth doing some research into what health insurance options are available to you before you give up a job that includes decent health coverage.

# 2  TAKING CARE OF BUSINESS

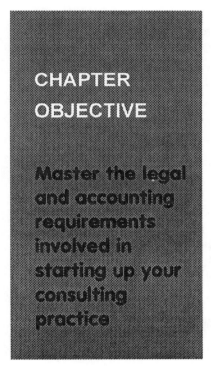

**CHAPTER OBJECTIVE**

Master the legal and accounting requirements involved in starting up your consulting practice

- Learn about the different legal forms under which you can do business

- Choose an effective business name and make it legal

- Take care of all required federal, state, and local taxes

- Find out about the insurance coverages that protect you and your business

- Review your office needs

At the outset of your consulting practice you must choose one of several possible forms of business under which to operate. This is because the way that your business will be taxed depends on its legal form. The forms of business available to independent small businesses are Sole Proprietor, Partnership, and various forms of incorporation. In addition, because of some fine print in the tax code that applies specifically to computer and engineering consultants, it is also possible that you will be forced to do your consulting work as an employee, rather than as any kind of independent businessperson.

If you don't take legal action to establish a partnership or corporation, and don't sign a contract that defines you as an employee, you automatically become a sole proprietorship. It costs no money to establish this status, and you are free to change the form of your business at any time in the future should your consulting practice grow to where some other option makes better economic sense.

It is almost always a waste of time and money to incorporate or set up any other complex legal structure for your business until you are sure you have a real business, with real clients and real income. Until then, sole proprietorship is an adequate form of business for almost all new consultants working on their own.

However, if you plan to begin consulting in association with another person, you need to talk to an accountant or tax attorney about incorporation immediately as partnership is not a safe form under which to do business.

> **LIABILITY?**
>
> Many successful consultants operate as sole proprietorships. New consultants worrying about personal liability should be reassured that liability suits against computer consultants are rare and the threat to personal assets minimal.
>
> If liability is a concern, limit it by incorporating or buy Errors and Omissions business insurance, discussed on Page 74.

## FACTS ABOUT SOLE PROPRIETORSHIP

If you don't take legal action you are automatically a sole proprietor. No legal steps or paperwork are required.

- Sole proprietors report their business income and expenses to the IRS on a Schedule C included with their federal tax return.

- There are no additional costs involved in maintaining sole proprietorship status.

- Sole proprietors may take a wide range of business deductions and establish Keogh and SEP retirement plans.

- Sole proprietors may deduct a percentage of their health insurance premiums from their taxes in those years when congress authorizes this deduction.

- If sued by a client, a sole proprietor's personal assets may be at stake.

## FACTS ABOUT PARTNERSHIP

Partnership is a legal status that must be defined by filing legal papers.

- When you are member of a partnership *all* your assets may be claimed by anyone who sues your partner for any reason—including his or her bad debts. This really does happen and has given partnerships a very bad reputation among consultants.

- If you insist on working in a partnership (particularly one with a spouse), be sure you specify in a formal partnership agreement what will happen to any partnership assets, goodwill, and client lists, in the event of an acrimonious split up.

> # GOTCHA!!
>
> Those who have tried it report that partnership has all the disadvantages of marriage and none of the rewards.
>
> Partnerships are usually begun by "close friends" and terminated by "sworn enemies."

## FACTS ABOUT INCORPORATION

Incorporation is a formal legal step that brings with it the need to fulfill specific government reporting and accounting requirements. Failure to fulfill these requirements may jeopardize your status as a corporation and result in heavy fines and penalties.

- The costs and benefits of various forms of incorporation vary from state to state.

- In some states small corporations are taxed more heavily than sole proprietorships. In others, they offer significant tax savings.

- If you are sued, incorporation *may* shield your personal assets, as those suing a corporation usually can only claim the assets of the corporation.

But this protection may disappearsif you can be shown to have incorporated for the purpose of avoiding liability when committing fraud or copyright infringement.

- If you incorporate but do not behave like a corporation, a claimant may also "pierce the corporate veil" and you will lose this protection.

- Incorporation should not be undertaken without consultation with a tax professional who specializes in small businesses and is familiar with the needs of computer consultants in your region.

- To find such a professional, get a referral from a satisfied local computer consultant.

- Unless you are working with other consultants, there is rarely any need to incorporate until you have been in business for a few years and have a good grasp of what your earnings and expenses will be.

---

## HOW DO YOU BECOME AN S-CORP?

When you incorporate you begin as a C-corporation.

You may switch to S-corporation status within 75 days of the start of your corporation's fiscal year.

You may switch back to C-corporation status at any time, but if you do you may not become an S-corporation again for five years.

S-corporations may offer tax advantages to small corporations with a limited number of owner-participants.

---

## S-CORPORATIONS AND C-CORPORATIONS

If you incorporate you must choose between one of two forms of incorporation and form an S-corporation or a C-corporation.

In a regular C-corporation, corporate income is taxed twice: once as corporate income and then again when the owner receives it as salary or dividends. In an S-corporation all corporate profits are passed through to the owners *untaxed* and then taxed as regular income. This is the primary reason closely-held companies with few owners choose to become S-corporations.

- Owners of S-corporations do not have to pay self-employment taxes on the income derived from the corporation unless they pay themselves a salary. However, if the corporation does not pay the owner a salary, no credit is accumulated towards Social Security benefits.

- S-corporations are limited in how they can do business outside of the U.S.

- S-corporations are limited as to how many stockholders they may have.

- Violating S-corporation rules may result in your company's losing its S-corporation status, being reclassified as a C-corporation and having to pay IRS penalties.

- S-corporations are not accepted in all states and are regulated and taxed punitively by others. It may be necessary to keep two different sets of books—one for Federal tax purposes and one for State tax purposes. It may also be necessary to pay taxes on the "earnings" of your S-corporation even when it has suffered a financial loss.

## FACTS ABOUT CONSULTING AS AN EMPLOYEE

Many consultants who work as contract programmers for larger corporations are forced to do their consulting as the employee of a consulting firm—even if they find their contracts on their own.

The reason for this has to do with the way the IRS defines employee status. The IRS provides a set of guidelines for distinguishing between employees and independent contractors (i.e., people running their own businesses.) These criteria are the "Twenty Questions for Establishing Independent Contractor Status."

> ### *Skip ahead if . . .*
>
> Consultants who don't plan to do the kind of consulting where they work on-site for clients for several weeks at a time, can ignore the next few pages and skip ahead to Page 57.

If you file your taxes as an independent contractor, but fail to meet the conditions defined by a significant number of these guidelines, the IRS may reclassify you as an employee of your client, whether or not you file your taxes as a sole proprietorship or corporation.

If this occurs, *clients* will be forced to pay payroll taxes on all the money they paid you and will also be assessed interest and penalties.

Because of their understandable fear of such a reclassification, many corporate clients have made it their policy to allow computer consultants to work on long-term, on-site contracts only if they are brought in as the W-2 employees of a third party consulting firm.

In some regions, clients will permit this "third party consulting firm" to be your own closely-held corporation. But in other parts of the country clients insist that you work as the employee of one of a limited number of "preferred vendors" which are almost always large consulting firm—often ones that have local reputations as "body shops."

## THE IMPACT OF SECTION 1706

*Q: My client mentioned something about "Section 1706" and said it meant I couldn't work for him as an independent contractor. What is he referring to?*

*A:* Section 1706 is a clause in the Tax Reform Act of 1986 which repeals a previous piece of tax legislation, Section 530 of the Revenue Act of 1978, which had exempted computer programmers and engineers from having to meet the stringent criteria the IRS uses to distinguish between employees and independent contractors. Without this exemption, computer consultants who want to be classified as independent contractors must meet the standards set by the IRS's "Twenty Questions for Establishing Independent Contractor Status."

*Q: Does Section 1706 repeal this exemption for all computer programmers and engineers?*

*A:* No. It is usually interpreted as applying only to these workers when they are working through a third party firm—i.e. a broker or consulting company.

*Q: I found a contract on my own, but a manager at the firm that wants to hire me told me that because of Section 1706 I couldn't work for them directly, even though a third party firm wasn't involved. What's going on here?*

*A:* Many corporate lawyers have interpreted the confusing wording of Section 1706 to apply to *any* contract worker and have advised their clients not to bring in such contractors except as W-2 employees of a large, established consulting firm with many employees.

## Q: Is there any chance that this legislation will be repealed soon?

**A:** There have been a few weak efforts to repeal Section 1706, including the commissioning of a study that demonstrated that the law is "revenue neutral"—i.e., that it doesn't increase the amount of taxes the government earns from contractors. However it is unlikely to be repealed. It has been in force for over eight years now, and the lobbying power of the large consulting firms who got it written into law in the first place is much greater than that of the poorly-organized transient population who make up the independent computer consultant community.

---

### Section 1706 of The Tax Reform Act of 1986

Here, in total, is the wording found in Section 1706 of the Tax Reform Act of 1986:

[Section 530] . . . "shall not apply in the case of an individual who, pursuant to an arrangement between the taxpayer and another person, provides services for such other person as an engineer, designer, drafter, computer programmer, systems analyst or other similarly skilled worker engaged in a similar line of work."

Clear as mud, eh?

# WORKSHEET: Are You An Employee Or An Independent Contractor?

*Use this questionnaire, adapted from the IRS "Twenty Questions," to decide whether your consulting practice meets the criteria for being treated as an independent contractor.*

## Answer each of the following with a "Yes" or "No" answer.

1. Does the client tell you what to do and how to do it?
   ☐ Yes ☐ No

2. Does the client provide training for you?
   ☐ Yes ☐ No

3. Are your services vital to your client staying in business?
   ☐ Yes ☐ No

4. Must you personally perform the work for the client?*

5. ☐ Yes ☐ No

6. Does the client hire and supervise workers who work as your assistants?
   ☐ Yes ☐ No

7. Is this a continuing relationship? Do you frequently work for this client over a long period of time?*
   ☐ Yes ☐ No

8. Do you have to work hours set by the client?
   ☐ Yes ☐ No

9. Must you work full-time for this client?
   ☐ Yes ☐ No

10. Must you work on the client's premises?
    ☐ Yes ☐ No

11. Must you perform your work in a sequence set by the client?
☐ Yes ☐ No

12. Must you submit regular oral or written reports to the client?*
☐ Yes ☐ No

13. Are you paid on a time and materials basis (i.e. using an hourly or daily rate plus expenses) rather than a fixed rate for the job?*
☐ Yes ☐ No

14. Does the client pay your travel or business expenses?*
☐ Yes ☐ No

15. Do you work on the client's equipment or using the client's tools?*
☐ Yes ☐ No

16. Have you no significant investment in your own business facilities and equipment?
☐ Yes ☐ No

17. Is it impossible for you to suffer a business loss because of the way your contracts are structured?
☐ Yes ☐ No

18. Do you work for only one client at a time?
☐ Yes ☐ No

19. Are your services not advertised to the general public?
☐ Yes ☐ No

20. Can the client terminate your contract unilaterally, even if you have produced results that meet the original contract specifications?
☐ Yes ☐ No

21. Can you terminate your contract unilaterally, even if the client has met the original contract obligations?
☐ Yes ☐ No

## UNDERSTANDING YOUR ANSWERS TO THE "Are You An Employee Or An Independent Contractor" WORKSHEET

"Yes" answers suggest that you are behaving like an employee, not an independent contractor. If you have given more than six "yes" answers, you might be in danger of being reclassified as an employee, rather than an independent contractor.

However, this is only a guideline. The IRS itself provides no actual information as to *how many* of these criteria must be met to qualify for independent status. Its publications merely suggest that if "employee" answers predominate, you are probably an employee.

Also, it's generally true that even the most defensibly independent computer consultants will have answer "Yes" to the items that are followed by asterisks (*) on the worksheet.

That is because, for reasons we'll be exploring in the next chapter, computer consultants customarily bill their clients on an hourly basis rather than quoting them fixed bids for many types of projects (as do lawyers in private practice, whose independent contractor status is unquestioned.)

For obvious reasons, too, computer consultants often find it necessary to work on the client's hardware with the client's software tools. So if these starred items are the only ones to which you have answered "Yes," don't worry.

## HOW TO MAINTAIN YOUR INDEPENDENCE

Here's how to maintain your independent contractor status:

- Work for several clients at one time

- Work on your own equipment at your own office as much as possible

- Refuse contracts that require you to work on-site 40 hours a week

- Retain the right to hire your own subcontractors and employees

- Pay for your own training

- Promote yourself to the public with PR and appropriate advertising

## GIVE YOUR BUSINESS A NAME

Once you've established a form for your business, you'll want to give it a name. This may require that you take care of some paperwork. This is because, in most jurisdictions, if you do not do business under your given name, you will need to file a form called a DBA. This acronym stands for, "Doing Business As." A DBA legally connects your business name with your personal name. (I.e., It defines your business as, "Joe Schmoe doing business as CompuGlitch.") This form is usually filed with your town clerk or at city hall. Call to find out what local requirements you must meet to register your business name.

## WORKSHEET: How Good Is Your Business Name?

*Use the following questionnaire to evaluate any name you choose for your business:*

1. Does the business name include your own name?

2. Have you checked to be sure that no other business in your region (or nationally) is already operating under this name?

3. Is the name easy to remember?

4. Is the name easy to pronounce?

5. Does the name remind potential clients of what it is you do?

6. If you were to expand your business or change your area of specialization, would you be forced to change your business name— as well as your stationary, cards, etc.?

7. Is the name "cute?" Will you get sick of that cuteness?

## COMMENTS ON BUSINESS NAMING

***INCLUDING YOUR PERSONAL NAME:*** In some jurisdictions if you include your last name in your business name, you do not have to file a DBA. Some consultants worry that a personal business name is unprofessional or labels them as "small time." However some of the nation's largest multi-partner consulting firms include a principal's name in their company names as do the names of most large accounting consulting firms.

***UNIQUENESS:*** While it is impossible to ensure that your business name is unique without having a lawyer do an expensive search, you can be pretty sure you've chosen a unique name if you don't find a similar name when you search a national database of business names and phone numbers. You can also try searching the on-line TrademarkScan database.

***PRONOUNCEABILITY:*** Ask friends to read your new business name off of a piece of paper to make sure that they pronounce it the way you intend it to be pronounced.

***MEMORABILITY:*** It might be useful if your business name reinforces the client's memory of what you do. But be careful not to choose a name that limits you to a very specific niche—for example, "Insurance Agency Systems"—if there is any chance you might want to expand out of that niche in the future. It is expensive for you and confusing to clients when you have to change an established business name.

***CUTENESS:*** If you choose a clever name, you might want to wait a week or two before committing to it, to make sure it is as clever as you originally thought.

***COMPU-ANYTHING:*** Try to avoid giving your company a name that sounds like ten thousand other computer consultancies. You *do* want people to be able to remember it.

***DON'T OBSESS:*** As many businesses succeed with awful names as fail with great ones. Do the best you can, and then forget it.

## SOAP BOX

Practice answering the question:

**"How Did You Come Up With The Name You Chose For Your Business?"**

Try to use your answer to get across your credential, specialty, or some other piece of information that will increase a client's interest in hiring you.

## BUSINESS LICENSES

Once you have your chosen your business name, you may need to apply for a business license.

Business licenses are issued locally. Call your town clerk or city hall to find out whether you need one and, if you do, what you must do to get one.

Usually business licenses are inexpensive. They typically cost around $20. However, the actual cost and other requirements you must meet depend on local laws and can vary greatly. Some localities do not even require that you have a business license.

## SET UP AN ACCOUNTING SYSTEM

### WHY AN ACCOUNTING SYSTEM?

As a sole proprietor you will be taxed only on your net income: what's left after you deduct your legitimate business expenses from the money your business has earned. So in order to pay your taxes properly, you will need to keep close track of your *income* (what clients pay you) and your *expenses* (what you spend in order to find and serve those clients.)

**NOTE—**

If you are incorporated, you will have to consult a tax professional to get accurate information about how to fulfill your accounting requirements.

## COMPUTERIZED ACCOUNTING SYSTEMS

There are many accounting software packages on the market designed for small businesses. Almost all of them can be used to track consulting income and expenses for tax purposes.

If you don't want to use canned software, you can set up your own accounting system by getting a copy of the IRS's Schedule C, "Profit and Loss from a Small Business," and IRS Publication 334 "Tax Guide for Small Businesses" and setting up a spreadsheet with categories that match the items listed on Schedule C and its associated forms.

## ACCOUNTING SOFTWARE RECOMMENDED FOR COMPUTER CONSULTANTS

Here are some of the software packages working consultants report using to handle their own accounting:

- Quicken

- Quickbooks

- MYOB for Windows

- One Write Plus

- ProfitWise

- BusinessWorks

While each of these packages has its strengths and weaknesses, what really counts is that you *use* whichever accounting package you get. So make sure you have some kind of accounting system in place *before* you spend a single cent on your business.

## KEEP BUSINESS MONEY SEPARATE FROM PERSONAL ACCOUNTS

Accountants recommend that even if you aren't incorporated, you get into the habit of keeping business income and expenses separate from personal income and expenses. To do this, open a separate savings and checking account for your business as soon as you have any business income.

Because business accounts can be expensive, shop around. Some banks will let you attach a second set of accounts to their premium savings/checking account packages at no additional cost. This is a much better deal than opening a formal business account which often requires that you pay hefty service fees.

## REMEMBER TO TRACK YOUR EXPENSES

The more expenses you can document the less taxes you'll pay. So keep alert.

- Save the receipts for any money you spend in the pursuit of business.

- Get into the habit of logging all expense items into your accounting system as soon as possible after they occur.

- Make sure you remember to log in any mileage you put on your car in the pursuit of business. Doing this can result in a significant tax deduction.

> **NOTE—**
>
> If you are forced to do your consulting contracts as a W-2 employee of a consulting firm (see discussion on Page 51) you can ignore this discussion. You will pay taxes as an employee and will be able to deduct only those expenses other employees can deduct.
>
> For more on deductible expenses, see Page 66.

## KEEP OUT OF TROUBLE WITH THE IRS

If you are operating as a sole proprietorship, when clients pay you they will not withhold any taxes from the money they send you. It is *your* responsibility to withhold tax payments from these checks and send them to the IRS.

> **NOTE—**
>
> If you work both as a W-2 consultant and as an independent consultant the advice in this section only applies to the income that your clients report to the IRS on a 1099 form.

At the end of the year clients will report the total amount they paid you on a form 1099. These forms go to the you, the IRS, and any state and local taxing authorities. The IRS will check the amounts on these forms against your tax return.

### HOW AND WHEN DO YOU PAY TAXES?

You must pay federal quarterly estimated tax withholding payments by April 15, July 15, Sept. 15, and Jan. 15. Consult state and local authorities for the dates you must meet to fulfill their tax withholding requirements.

- To get federal quarterly tax withholding forms, including a worksheet you can use to estimate what you will owe, call **800-829-3676**

- To get a Federal Tax ID number, call **800-829-1040**
  A Federal Tax ID is *not* required if you are sole proprietor, have no employees and do not collect sales tax. In that case you can simply file using your social security number.

- To get state tax withholding forms contact your state's taxing authority. You can usually find a telephone number for it in the White Pages listed under the name of your state.

- If your city levies an income tax, call to find out if city income tax quarterly payments are required.

- If you receive income from clients in several states, you will have to pay income taxes to each of these states. If this is your situation, keep impeccable records and consult an accountant to make sure you comply with all applicable laws.

### HOW MUCH MUST YOU PAY TO AVOID PENALTIES?

IRS regulations provide that you must withhold either an amount equal to what you paid in taxes last year or 90% of this year's actual tax liability.

## BUSINESS PROPERTY TAXES

Some states allow local jurisdictions to tax business property including computers and other office machinery. Call your town clerk or city hall to find out if this is the case where you operate your business, and what you must do to comply.

## DON'T TAKE CHANCES WITH TAXES

If you are not sure you understand how to comply with these tax requirements, find an accountant and let them advise you. If you mess up when paying your taxes it can end up costing you far more than the cost of having an accountant do the work. A good accountant should also be able to give you other useful business advice.

> # GOTCHA!!
>
> Besides withholding for income taxes, you must also withhold 15.3% of the first $60,000 you earn for Self-Employment Tax as well as 2.5% of the amount above $60,000.
>
> This is in addition to Federal Income Tax and covers Social Security and Medicare payments.

But it is important that any tax professional you rely on be one who already works with other consultants whose businesses and income levels are similar to your own. An accountant who is not used to dealing with businesses similar to yours may give you advice that would be good advice for different kind of business, but poor advice for yours.

# WHAT YOU HAVE TO KNOW ABOUT SALES TAXES

### WHEN IS SALES TAX COLLECTED?

If you intend to sell hardware or packaged software to clients, you may need to obtain a state sales tax certificate (sometimes called a "reseller's certificate") or some equivalent document from your state taxing authority.

When buying wholesale, you'll give the wholesaler the number of your reseller's certificate to avoid paying tax on items you will be reselling to clients. When you sell an item to a client, you charge them the sales tax, which you send to the state at some specified time. You will still have to pay taxes on any items you buy wholesale but keep for your own use.

Before you sell anything to clients, you will need to find out exactly which goods and services are taxable in your state. This varies widely from state to state. In particular, you'll want to find out whether sales of customized software, shrink-wrapped software, and computer hardware are taxed in your state. In addition, some states also apply sales taxes to the delivery of pure services, so you'll need to check into whether this is true in the states where you will be doing business.

Some municipalities also levy sales taxes. Find out if this is the case in your city and if it is, be sure you remember to collect these taxes and pay them to the city at the appropriate time.

## TAX CHECKLIST

☐ Find out when your next Federal, State, and City estimated withholding payments are due. Write date here: _____

☐ Put a note on your calendar two weeks before this date to remind yourself to make these payments if they are necessary.

☐ Call up now and request Federal, State, and Local estimated tax withholding forms for any jurisdictions in which you expect to earn income this year.

☐ Call State and Local taxing authorities in any state in which you plan to do business and request information about what goods and services are taxable in their jurisdiction.

☐ Apply for a sales tax certificate if you will be selling any taxable items.

☐ Note the date your next State and/or City sales tax payment is due. Write it here: _____

☐ Put a system in place to track all taxable sales you make to clients and make sure you record all taxable sales in a timely manner.

☐ Find out if there are any local property taxes assessed against business property and remember to set aside money to pay them.

☐ Begin calling local accountants and interview several until you find one with whom you feel comfortable.

Obviously, it is essential that you keep excellent records of any sales you make to clients. You may find it useful to keep track of these sales using Time and Billing software which you'll find described in Chapter Eight.

### HOW AND WHEN TO PAY SALES TAXES

- Each state has its own regulations about how and when you must turn over the sales taxes you collect.

- Usually, the more taxes you collect, the more frequently you must pay the taxes.

- Mail order sales to buyers in states other than those where your business is physically located are usually not subject to tax.

- If you do business in several states—in person, rather than by mail—you will have to comply with the sales taxes that apply in *each* state in which you operate.

- If you find this confusing, consult an accountant.

## DEDUCTIBLE BUSINESS EXPENSES

One of the great advantages of being an independent contractor is that you pay taxes only on the income that remains after you have deducted legitimate business expenses. This makes it very important that you remember to track these expenses.

Here is a list of some of the more common expenses consultants deduct. Though some of them may look trivial, over the course of a year they may amount to several hundred dollars.

### TAX DEDUCTIONS FOR CONSULTANTS

- Accountants' fees
- Admission to business events and meetings
- Attorneys' fees
- Banking fees for your business accounts
- Books, both business and professional
- Brochures, design and printing costs
- Business cards, design and printing costs
- Classes and seminars you take to enhance your professional skills
- Computer equipment

- Copier, purchase or rental
- Copying expenses
- Fax machine
- Food and entertainment for clients (50%)
- Insurance premiums for business insurance
- Licenses and permits
- Long distance charges listed on your home phone bill
- Membership fees for joining professional groups (but NOT club dues)
- Mileage for any work-related travel, including trips to the post office to mail letters and to the library to do research
- Office supplies (paper, pens, printer ribbons, toner, folders, staplers, etc.)
- On-line service monthly fees and connect charges
- Phone and Fax line monthly service charges
- Postage, Fedex, and UPS shipping charges
- Professional journal and trade magazine subscriptions
- Software you buy for use in your business
- Stationary

## ACCOUNTING FOR SOFTWARE PURCHASES

When you do your taxes there are several different ways to account for software that you buy for your own use:

- Software that comes installed with a new computer may be treated as part of the computer and the entire purchase may be written off as a one time Section 179 expense—up to a limit of $17,500 per year. Hardware purchases over that amount must be depreciated over a period of 5 years.

- Cheap software packages—whose costs the IRS defines as "immaterial" compared to your total business income—may be expensed and put in the "supplies" category. In practice this applies to software costing under $100 for most consultants, though some consultants with high incomes report expensing packages costing up to $250.

- More expensive software you buy for your own use must be depreciated as a 3-year intangible asset.

- Software you buy for future sale to clients is treated as inventory.

## THE HOME OFFICE DEDUCTION

The Home Office Deduction is a special deduction. Claiming it requires that you meet several criteria. Answer the following questions to determine if you can claim a home office deduction.:

### CAN YOU CLAIM A HOME OFFICE TAX DEDUCTION?

1. Do you have a separate room in your house you use only for business purposes?

2. Do you NOT have another office available for your use, anywhere else?

3. After you deduct all your other expenses, will you still report more income than you plan to deduct with your home office deduction?

4. Are you aware that claiming a home office deduction may increase your likelihood of experiencing an IRS audit?

If you answered "Yes" to the first three questions, you can claim a home office deduction. You do this by filling in a special form, IRS Form 8829, "Expenses for Business Use of your Home" when you file your taxes.

If you don't have enough income to claim a home office deduction you can file form 8829 anyway, and deduct the home office expenses you incurred this year in a future year when you have more income.

Make sure your home office is in compliance with local zoning laws. This is particularly important if clients come to your home and park in the street where they may annoy neighbors. You don't want the town shutting your business down.

## GOTCHA!!

By claiming a home office deduction you are converting a portion of your home to business use.

Therefore, if you have been claiming a home office deduction for a portion of your home, when you sell that home you may not be able to roll over the portion of the capital gain from the sale that corresponds to the portion that you have been treating as a business property.

In that case you will have to pay Federal and State income taxes on the business portion of the gain, which can amount to many thousands of dollars.

In order to avoid this, consult with an accountant to find out how you can convert the business portion of your home back to a residence before putting it on the market.

## HOW MUCH TAX DO YOU REALLY PAY?

Talk of "tax brackets" can be misleading if you don't take into account the tax deductions and exemptions that your business may claim. How much of your consulting dollar you'll actually pay in taxes may also depend on how much your spouse earns.

Here are some examples to give you a general idea of how much of what you earn you can expect to keep. These examples are figured using 1995 tax formulas.

When estimating your taxes, don't forget to include state income taxes too. These may easily add another 3-6% to your tax burden.

## HOW BIG IS THE FEDERAL TAX BITE?

To give you an idea of how much tax you will really pay on your consulting dollars, we've provided three different scenarios that show how much tax would be taken out of the same consulting income given various family configurations.

In all the following examples assume:

Gross Income from Consulting:........... $50,000
Expenses Deducted from Income:......... <u>15,000</u>
Net Income from Consulting ................. 35,000

### EXAMPLE 1: *Married, Two Children, Nonworking Spouse*

Federal Tax................................................$2,767.50
(15% of what is left after
deducting the standard deduction
for married filing jointly and four
personal exemptions.)

Federal Self Employment Tax.......................5,355.00
(Straight 15.3% of taxable
income.)

TOTAL.......................................................... $8,122.50

ACTUAL FEDERAL TAX BITE: 23%

## EXAMPLE 2: Married, Two Children, Working Spouse Earning A Salary Of $50,000

Federal Tax on consulting income................ $5,166.00
   (Treating the consulting income as
   the second family income,
   consulting Income is taxed at 28%
   after subtracting the standard
   deduction for married filing jointly
   and four personal exemptions.)

Federal Self Employment Tax ...................... 5,355.00
on Consulting Income
   (Straight 15.3% of taxable
   income.)

TOTAL ...................................................... $10,521.00

ACTUAL FEDERAL TAX BITE: 30%

## EXAMPLE 3: Single, No Dependents

Federal Income Tax..................................... $4,972.50
   (15% of net after deducting
   standard deduction for single. and
   one personal exemption.)

Federal Self-Employment Tax...................... 5,355.00
   (Straight 15.3% of taxable
   income.)

TOTAL ...................................................... $10,327.50

ACTUAL FEDERAL TAX BITE: 30%

## OFFICE AND BUSINESS EQUIPMENT QUESTIONS

### Q: Do I need to rent a professional-looking office before I contact a client?

**A:** No. One of the biggest mistakes new consultants make is to invest a lot of time and money in the trappings of their businesses before their businesses *are* in business.

Many very successful computer consultants work out of home offices. Clients are much more likely to be impressed by your credentials and list of past projects than they are by your address or office furniture.

### Q: Are there advantages to leasing a car for my business?

**A:** There may be advantages to leasing a car, but again, there's no need to worry about this until you've been in business for a while and demonstrated that you can earn enough income to make this kind of arrangement pay off. If you have reached that point, consult an accountant to see if leasing makes sense in your particular tax and business situation.

### Q: Up until now, I've done all my work on a computer at work. Don't I need to buy my own computer?

**A:** If you don't already have your own computer, you probably are not ready to set yourself up as a computer consultant—unless you plan to specialize exclusively in mainframe or mid-range system work. Most successful consultants already own sophisticated business computer systems at the time they begin their practices. This reflects the dedication with which they've approached improving their computer skills and keeping current with technology.

### Q: What about upgrading my home system?

**A:** Unless there's a demonstrable business need, wait until you have real clients before you invest in expensive new hardware and software. You should already own the software you consider yourself an "expert" in. Remember, business deductions aren't worth anything to you if you don't have business income.

## TYPES OF BUSINESS INSURANCE COVERAGE

Review the following list of types of business insurance to familiarize yourself with the kinds of insurance your business may need.

Before you purchase any insurance, ask other local business people to recommend capable local independent insurance agents or call a selection of local independent insurance agents on your own and ask them to explain to you the benefits of the different plans they sell.

Do your best to keep costs low, but remember that bad insurance can be worse than no insurance if it lulls you into a false sense of security.

### *GENERAL LIABILITY:*

***WHAT IT COVERS:*** Bodily injury you cause to others. Property damage you cause to the property of others. Personal injury and advertising injury arising out of the operation of your business.

***WHEN IT COVERS:*** Claims are covered only for losses that occur during the period during which the policy is in force.

***HOW MUCH DOES IT COVER:*** Policies are written with a "per occurrence" limit—usually $300,000, $500,000 or $1,000,000.

***WHAT IT DOES NOT COVER:*** Damage to "intangibles" like a client's data and, depending on specific exclusions that are often written into GL policies, it *may also not* cover:

- Any claims for damages that do not occur at your business premises.

- Professional liability of any kind.

- Claims outside of the U.S. and its territories.

- Libel, slander, etc..

***WHO NEEDS IT:*** Consultants who run storefront retail establishments or work on client equipment in their own offices.

***ADDITIONAL COMMENTS:*** If you worry about being sued for dropping the client's laptop computer, this is the policy for you. Unfortunately, because of a fear that they will end up having to pay claims for damage your computer programs cause, many insurers won't write GL coverage for computer consultants. When they do write it, they tend exclude just about any coverage you might be able to use. Most computer consultants only buy this coverage if clients demand they have it.

## ERRORS & OMISSIONS COVERAGE

**WHAT IT COVERS:** Damages caused by your professional negligence while programming, installing, configuring, and using computers for a client. Your legal defense against lawsuits, justified and frivolous, brought by clients.

**WHEN DOES IT COVER:** Unless prior acts are excluded, this kind of policy will cover all claims that are brought during the terms of the policy for losses that may have occurred during or *before* the period of coverage. Since such a policy covers every professional act you've performed from the beginnings of your business it can be *very* expensive.

**HOW IS IT WRITTEN:** Many insurers will figure your premium based on the amount of annual income you earn in your business. Obviously this can pose a problem if you are just starting out.

**WHAT IT DOES NOT COVER:**

- Fraud.
- Criminal acts.
- Wrongful acts committed prior to writing the policy.
- Wrongful transfer of funds
- Copyright infringement.

**WHO NEEDS IT:** Consultants whose clients demand that they have it. Otherwise, incorporation is probably as good a defense against lawsuits. Some attorneys even warn that having this kind of insurance is likely to encourage clients to sue.

**COMMENTS:** You can often find better rates on this kind of insurance through a professional organization serving professionals in your field. If a client insists that you have this type of insurance coverage, you should make sure that the amount they pay you for the job covers the premium you'll have to pay.

## EDP COVERAGE

**WHAT IT COVERS:** Computers, software. Damage from power surges, earthquakes, in-transit damage. Some policies may cover interruptions to your business due to loss of computers.

**WHERE DO YOU GET IT:** Specialized insurers including Safeware, St. Paul, Atlantic Mutual, or Northbrook.

**WHAT TO WATCH OUT FOR:** Exclusions for power surges.

**WHO SHOULD HAVE IT:** All computer owners.

### GOTCHA!!

Don't assume that your computers and other home office equipment are covered under your homeowner's or renter's policy. They are almost always excluded.

## BUSINESS PROPERTY COVERAGE

**WHAT IT COVERS:** Damage to your business property including your office, computers, and (within limits) the goods of others that are temporarily left on your premises (including computers you repair.)

**WHEN IT COVERS:** While the policy is in force.

**HOW MUCH DOES IT COVER:** The amount of your claim minus a deductible, up to the amount you insure. However, if you file a claim and are found to have under-insured your property, you may only collect a proportion of the claim, rather than the full amount of damage minus the deductible. So you must make sure you adequately estimate the value of your property.

**WHAT IT MAY NOT COVER:**

Depending on specific clauses and exclusions that are common in this type of policy, Business Property Coverage may not cover:

- Damage from floods or earthquakes.
- Property of others left on your premises over a low limit ($2,500).
- Goods in transit (i.e. computers in your van or someone else's).

- Software and specialized computer equipment damaged by power failures and viruses.

**WHO SHOULD HAVE IT:** Anyone with a significant investment in non-computer business property.

## DISABILITY INSURANCE

**WHAT IT COVERS:** Disability insurance pays you a monthly income should you become too ill or disabled to continue working at your business. The amount of this income is defined in the policy and based on the actual income you have been earning from your business.

**WHEN DOES IT COVER:** You will have to be disabled for a predetermined period of time before the policy begins to pay you a monthly payment. The longer the period you are willing to wait before declaring yourself disabled and claiming payment, the lower your premium.

**WHAT DOES IT NOT COVER:**

- Disability due to drug abuse or self-inflicted injuries.

- Disability due to pre-existing conditions that you did not disclose on your application for the policy.

**WHAT TO WATCH OUT FOR:**
Policies that define "disability" as an inability to perform "any occupation" rather than "the duties of your occupation." Policies that treat money owing to you but not collected (or even collectible) as "income" when figuring your benefit.

**WHO SHOULD HAVE IT:** All computer consultants, as soon as they qualify for it. If you wait until you have a sickness or accident it's too late to buy this coverage.

**COMMENTS:** If you are just starting out as an independent contractor you may only be able to get disability

### GOTCHA!!

If your policy defines disability as being unable to perform any occupation and you had an accident that left you brain-damaged and unable to read, you might be denied coverage as the insurer could argue that you could still dig ditches.

Make sure that your policy defines disability as an inability to perform the customary duties of your occupation.

insurance after you have been in business for several years and can document the amount of income you earn from your business. This is because the benefit a disability policy will pay is calculated as a percentage of your income from your business. W-2 consultants can often get coverage immediately based on their earnings as W-2 employees in previous years.

## HEALTH INSURANCE

**WHAT IT COVERS:** Visits to the doctor, emergency room, hospital, surgery, drugs, etc..

**WHEN IT COVERS:** During the term of the policy.

**WHAT IT DOES NOT COVER:** A bewildering number of situations, which are different for each policy, insurer, and state.

**WHO SHOULD HAVE IT:** Anyone with assets like a home or savings account who does not have a written statement signed by God attesting that they will never have a unexpected serious accident or illness. Remember, a single hospitalization can easily cost you $200,000.

**COMMENTS:** There are two kinds of health policies available to consultants: individual policies which are available to anyone and group policies which are written for businesses or individuals who meet certain conditions—though the sole condition you may have to meet may be membership in the group.

Typically, the policies that are available to businesses that have less than three employees offer less comprehensive coverage than those that cover companies with three or more full-time employees. Incorporation in and of itself will not improve your ability to buy effective insurance as it is the number of employees, not the company's tax status that defines which plans will be offered.

## A GARLAND OF HEALTH INSURANCE GOTCHAS

❧ If you have a group business policy, you may lose your coverage if your group has a higher than usual number of claims and the insurer decides to cancel their coverage of the group.

❧ If you have a company insurance plan that covers you as an employee, the law may require you to cover any other employees you may hire in the future.

❧ If you *or any member of your family* have a pre-existing condition, including such relatively benign conditions as asthma, many insurers will refuse you coverage. Make sure you can get health insurance on your own before you give up coverage from an old employer's plan or a spouse's job.

❧ HMOs and other plans that limit you to specific doctors and hospitals may keep you (or a family member) from getting the treatment you need from doctors at a nationally recognized medical center should you come down with an obscure disease that is difficult to diagnose or treat. If you don't think this could be a problem for you, remember that no one plans to come down with these kinds of diseases.

❧ When you apply for health, life or disability insurance, insurers may ask for a list of your doctors and investigate your medical history for the past five to ten years. Some insurers will require that you give their representatives blood and urine samples.

❧ Health insurance scams abound. Be wary of groups claiming to be business or professional groups that tout their insurance plans as the main benefit of joining, particularly if they do not hold local or regional meetings or annual conventions. These organizations are frequently fronts for sleazy insurance companies or outfits that sell expensive but useless directory listings to the newly self-employed.

## ESTABLISH CREDIT WITH VENDORS

If you plan to buy hardware and software wholesale for resale to clients you'll need to establish credit with the vendors you plan to order from. Otherwise you will have to pay by check—and wait for the check to clear—or COD.

Once you establish credit with a wholesaler or vendor, you will billed monthly and will be expected to pay within 30 days of receiving the invoice.

To establish credit with a wholesaler or vendor you will need to obtain a state reseller's certificate (discussed on Page 64.) If you live in a state that doesn't have a sales tax and hence doesn't issue reseller's certificates you may be able to substitute a Federal Tax ID number for the resale certificate. You will also need to have a clean personal credit history.

Even if you have a good credit rating, not all vendors will give you credit, so you may have to hunt around until you find ones who will. Your initial credit limit will probably be low—$500 to $1,500—but as you become a steady customer, you should be able to get it raised. Once you establish solid credit with one vendor, you may be able to use that information to get credit with others.

# TAKING CARE OF BUSINESS CHECKLIST

HAVE YOU:

☐ Chosen the form of business under which you will operate?

☐ Sent away for federal, state, and city quarterly withholding forms?

☐ Estimated your taxable income and reminded yourself when to pay quarterly payments?

☐ Established an accounting system or found a good accountant to handle complex tax issues?

☐ Found out if you need a state or city sales tax certificate?

☐ Filed the appropriate forms if you do?

☐ Chosen a business name?

☐ Made sure your business name is unique?

☐ Filed a DBA if necessary?

☐ Gotten any required business licenses?

☐ Insured your computers?

☐ Discussed other insurance needs with a reputable agent?

☐ Looked into establishing credit with vendors?

# 3 HOW TO SET YOUR RATE

**CHAPTER OBJECTIVE**

Learn the methods computer consultants use to set their rates and choose the one that best fits your personal style

- Understand how to use fixed bids and hourly rates
- Determine how to set a fair hourly rate
- Discover how to bill for travel and other extras
- Find out how to use retainers
- Understand what's involved in taking credit cards
- Know when to offer discounts and when to raise your rates

"How much do you charge?" will inevitably be among any prospect's first questions to you. If you don't have an answer ready, you will mark yourself as an amateur. But if you give a price without thinking through the consequences, you may end up working for free—or even losing money on the contract. So you need to decide how you are going to bill before you approach potential clients.

## Q: What is the best way to bill clients for my services?

**A:** There is no one answer that will fit all consultants. You must take into account your experience level, specialty, and the billing methods used by other consultants in your niche. But you will probably have to choose some version of one of the two main methods commonly used to bill for consulting work: 1) Charging an *Hourly Rate*, sometimes described as billing for "Time and Materials," or 2) Presenting a *Fixed Bid*.

# FIXED BIDS

### HOW THE FIXED BID METHOD OF BILLING WORKS

The client describes their needs to the consultant who then proposes to do the job for a set dollar amount. In theory, this amount is arrived at by estimating the hours needed to complete the job and multiplying those hours by the consultant's target hourly rate. If the bid is accepted, the consultant is legally obligated to deliver whatever they have promised for the stated amount, no matter how much extra time the project actually requires.

### WHY CLIENTS LIKE A FIXED BID

Many clients—particularly those who do not have much experience working with computer consultants—prefer fixed bids because:

- There are no "ugly surprises" when it is time to pay.

- Costs can be budgeted.

- It calms their fears that the consultant will work slowly to run up a big bill.

### WHY SOME CONSULTANTS LIKE FIXED BIDS

Consultants who use fixed bids successfully prefer them because:

- They can complete a project in less time than the client expects it to take. Thus they can earn more than they could when working at an hourly rate.

- When their estimates are correct, they get rewarded for efficiency.

- When their estimates are correct, they get rewarded for reusing existing code and reapplying solutions from other projects.

## WHY MOST CONSULTANTS DREAD FIXED BIDS

The many experienced consultants who have lost money on fixed bid jobs—often a great deal of money—warn against them because:

- It is almost impossible to estimate the costs of a computer project accurately early in the development cycle. But this is when clients are most likely to want a fixed bid. The rule of thumb for such situations is "Make your best guess and multiply it by three." But self-confident consultants rarely use such a realistic fudge factor and often end up making over-optimistic bids that end up costing them money.

- In competitive bidding situations where the low bidder wins the job, unrealistic estimates abound and it is almost impossible to win with an accurate estimate.

- Computer consulting projects usually involve working with bleeding edge technologies prone to bugs and other nasty surprises that cannot be easily factored into time estimates.

- Completing the project may depend on the efforts of client employees and of vendors whose performance is out of the consultant's control.

- Clients who are vague about their exact requirements still insist on getting a fixed bid for their projects. When the requirements are later defined, even if they are substantially different from the description the bid was based on, clients often expect the client to stick with the price stated in the original bid.

- Clients love to change the spec in mid-project but usually resist renegotiating the cost of the fixed bid.

- Fixed bid contracts may make it impossible to make needed changes in the middle of a project because clients resist increasing the project's cost.

## *PROJECT THAT ARE APPROPRIATE FOR FIXED BIDS*

You're more likely to come out ahead quoting a fixed bid in the following situations:

1.  Projects using *known and proven technologies* with which you are extremely familiar.

    > **Example:** The client wants you to install and support an accounting system for a retail store. You have already installed twenty-seven such systems in the past.

2.  Situations in which a *"canned" product* is being sold.

    > **Example:** The client wants to buy and install a package designed to manage a video rental store and agrees that any modifications to the system will not be included in the price of the installation.

3.  Situations in which the deliverable is a *report* or *specification*.

    > **Example:** The client wants to know what it would take to put his company on the Internet. He agrees to pay you a flat rate to do a study, the final result of which will be a report listing various methods of accomplishing this goal and each method's estimated costs.

---

### NEVER QUOTE A FIXED BID WHEN . . .

- The client is not sure exactly what he or she needs done.
- You will be dependent on the work of people not under your control.
- You have never done this kind of project before.
- You are implementing bleeding edge technology.
- You can't afford to lose money on the project.

## HOW TO PROTECT YOURSELF WHEN MAKING FIXED BIDS

- Quote a fixed bid for creating a project specification and bid on the completed project only when the specification is accepted.

- Break the project up into phases and bid only on one phase at a time.

- Make it clear that if the spec changes, the rate for subsequent work must be renegotiated.

- Design your contract so that you get paid substantial amounts at several points throughout the project, not just at the end.

- Build checkpoints into the project at which the rate may be renegotiated if conditions have changed significantly.

- Make sure your client understands that a fixed rate does not guarantee that you will deliver on time if you are dependent on factors outside of your control.

- Make sure there is some way of modifying or terminating the contract if conditions and assumptions change radically.

- Keep detailed time and expense records of all projects you complete and use these to improve the accuracy of your estimates.

# HOURLY RATES

## *HOW THE HOURLY METHOD OF BILLING WORKS*

The consultant bills the client a set amount for each hour worked. Invoices are sent to the client for work already done at an agreed-upon interval and the client is expected to pay these invoices within a reasonable amount of time. If too many invoices go unpaid, the consultant may stop work on the project.

## *WHY CLIENTS ACCEPT HOURLY RATES*

The Hourly Rate method is the billing method most frequently used by experienced computer consultants. This is particularly true when dealing with assignments that are expected to last more than a week. Clients accept this method of billing because:

- It is an industry standard and few high-quality consultants will accept any other arrangement.

- The large consulting companies that provide the majority of consultants to corporate clients almost always bill on an hourly basis.

- Clients have confidence in the ability and ethics of the consultants they hire.

- Clients understand that it is impossible for any consultant to make accurate time estimates for large projects that depend on the combined efforts of many developers and vendors.

- Clients are accustomed to paying other professionals such as attorneys and accountants on an hourly basis.

## WHY CONSULTANTS LIKE HOURLY RATES

Most consultants prefer to bill their services at an hourly rate because when they do:

- Problems caused by forces outside their control do not cost them money.

- They do not have to fight with the client every time a change is needed in the project specification.

- It is easier to convince clients to prioritize their needs and make it clear what should be done first and what can be postponed or allowed to slide.

- They don't have to worry about getting trapped in money-losing projects.

- They can more easily estimate how many hours they will have available to sell to other clients.

- Invoices are kept relatively small which makes them easier for clients to pay, unlike the much larger lump sums that characterize payment for fixed bids.

- They can more easily cut their losses and abandon a project if the client turns out to be one who has no intention of paying.

## HOURLY RATES ARE APPROPRIATE FOR:

- Contract programming projects.

- On-going support for existing systems, both on-site and by phone.

- Training classes and individual training sessions.

- Any project involving implementation of brand new technologies.

- Any work done for corporate MIS departments.

## WORKSHEET: Fixed Bid Or Hourly

*Use the following worksheet to decide which kind of rate is best for a given project:*

1. Have you done a project very similar to this one before?

   ☐Yes  ☐No


2. Does the client have a detailed, written specification?

   ☐Yes  ☐No


3. Will the client agree to renegotiate the project cost if the specification changes?

   ☐Yes  ☐No


4. Have you done a successful project with this client before and found the client honest and easy to deal with?

   ☐Yes  ☐No


5. Can you get paid a significant amount of money up front?

   ☐Yes  ☐No

6. Can you get paid interim payments throughout the project?

☐Yes ☐No

7. Can you afford it if the project takes twice as long as your worst case estimate?

☐Yes ☐No

8. Will your deadlines be dependent on the work of client employees?

☐Yes ☐No

9. Will you be working with unknown software or hardware?

☐Yes ☐No

10. Will you be dependent on a product now undergoing Beta testing?

☐Yes ☐No

11. Will you be relying on subcontractors to complete this project?

☐Yes ☐No

## SCORING THE FIXED BID VS. HOURLY RATE WORKSHEET

If all answers to questions 1–7 are "yes" and all answers to questions 8–11 are "no" you can consider bidding a fixed bid for this project.

If you answered "no" to questions 1 or 7, or "yes" to questions 8, 9, or 10, you face very high risks if you take this project on a fixed bid basis.

If you answered "no" questions 2, 3, 5, or 6, only consider doing this project on a fixed bid basis if you can negotiate with the client to get a written contract that allows you to answer "yes" to each of these questions.

## RETAINERS

A billing method frequently associated with the term "consultant" is "working on retainer."

Many retainer arrangements are nothing more than another way of structuring an hourly rate arrangement. With this kind of retainer, the client pays in advance for *a set number of hours*. After these hours are used up, any additional hours that the consultant works are billed to the client at a rate specified in the original retainer agreement.

Another form of retainer is one in which the consultant provides a service like network maintenance to a client for *a set monthly fee*. In this case, the fee is the same whether the consultant is on-site daily or visits once a month. Obviously, this kind of retainer should only be entered into if the work involved meets the guidelines set out above for any fixed bid project.

Consultants who use retainers often give their clients a discounted rate on the hours involved to give the client an incentive to book those hours in advance.

### UNUSED HOURS

One big question posed by a retainer arrangement that obliges you to work for a fixed number of hours is this: What do you do if the client hasn't used up all the contracted hours when the retainer expires?

- Some consultants allow clients to carry over the unused hours into a new retainer period.

- Others treat all hours as expired when the retainer expires.

Which solution you chose will probably depend on how busy you are and how likely you are to fill your billable hours with other, perhaps more highly paid, work. But make sure you know what your policy will be before you offer a client a retainer arrangement.

## WHAT ARE TODAY'S CONSULTANTS CHARGING?

On Page 92 you'll find the results of a survey of rates collected from members of Compuserve's Computer Consultants Forum. This information is presented to give you a sense of what real rates are like. Study these rates and note how they vary depending on the technology involved, the consultant's credentials, the length of the assignment, the geographical location of the job, and whether or not a third party (broker) firm is involved.

### Key to Terms Used in Table 3.

| TERM | |
|---|---|
| **Brokered** | The consultant was placed by a broker or is a subcontractor or W-2 non-benefited hourly rate consultant working for a consulting firm. |
| **Dev't** | Software development work. |
| **F100** | The consultant was employed as a Fortune 100 MIS employee. |
| **Home** | Work is performed mainly at the consultant's home or office. |
| **On-site** | Work is performed mainly at the clients' offices. |
| **Rate/hr** **Rate/day** | These are the amounts the consultant earns. In brokered situations the actual rate paid by the client is higher than the rate cited here. |
| **Remote** | The consultant works from home for clients in other parts of the country via modem. |
| **Travel** | The consultant travels to client sites in distant parts of the country. |

## Table 3. Real Consulting Rates 1994-1995

| Specialty | Location | Rate/hr | Rate/day | Brokered | Length | Experience |
|---|---|---|---|---|---|---|
| Analysis, Govt | DC | $60 | | No | <6 wks | MBA/CPA |
| Analysis, Insurance | NJ | $100 | | No | <6 mo | MBA/CPA |
| Analysis, Mfg | NJ | $80 | | No | <6 wks | MBA/CPA |
| ASM/C/C++/Embedded Systems | N. Cal | $75 | | No | 40 days/yr | |
| Assembly/DOS/Windows Dev't | East Coast/Remote | $75 | | No | 1-3 mos | Ex-vendor engineer |
| BAL/MVS | Dallas | $55 | | No | Long-term | |
| Business Analyst | DC | $60-80 | | | <2 mos | CPA |
| Business Process Reengineering | NYC | $100-150 | | | <2 mos | CPA |
| C++ | Springfield, MA | $60 | | Yes | 6 mos | |
| C/C++ Programming/Support | N. Cal | $60 | | No | 1 yr/53 hrs/wk | |
| Client Server/Business Analyst | NYC | $80-125 | | | <2 mos | CPA |
| Client Server Dev't/Multi-platform | NY/NJ (own office) | $105-150 | | No | wks-yrs | 10+ F100 |
| COBOL | Dallas | $50 | | No | | |
| COBOL II/MVS | Dallas | $55 | | No | Long-term | |
| COBOL/Mainframe | NYC (on-site) | $50 | | | Long-term | |
| COBOL Programming | DC | $80-100 | | No | Long-term | |
| Database/Pharmaceutical/Biotech | Idaho/Travel/Remote | $75 | | | | |
| DB/2/COBOL | St. Louis | $28 | | Yes | 6 mos | |
| DB/2/Microfocus COBOL | Hartford | $38 | | Yes | 6 mos | |
| Delrina Form Flow | Travel | $120 | | No | 6.5 hrs, 36 hrs | |
| Drivers/Communications /ASM/C++ | | $60-75 | | Yes | 7 mos | |
| Drivers/Communications /ASM/C++ | | $75 | | No | 4 mos | |
| Embedded Systems/PC Interfaces | S.Cal | $125+ long dist. travel expenses | | No | 18 mos | Ph.D. EE |
| Embedded Systems/PC | S.Cal | $75+long dist. | | No | 18 mos | EE |

| Specialty | Location | Rate/hr | Rate/day | Brokered | Length | Experience |
|---|---|---|---|---|---|---|
| Interfaces | | travel expenses | | | | |
| Factory Automation | N. Carolina/Travel | | | Yes | | |
| Factory Automation | Travel | | $550 | Yes | | |
| Forth, Trading System | NJ | $50-70 | | Yes | 2 yrs. | |
| FoxPro | Denver | $30 | | No | 1-8 hrs | |
| FoxPro | Denver | $34 | | Yes | <8 hrs | |
| FoxPro | Hartford | $25 | | Yes | 6 mos/part-time | |
| FoxPro | LA | $30-35 | | Yes | 2-5 mos | |
| FoxPro | NY/NJ (home) | | | | | |
| FoxPro | NY/NJ (on-site) | $69 | | | 15 mos | |
| FoxPro | Orlando (home) | $75 | $750 | | | 10+ years indep. |
| FoxPro | S.Cal | $45 | | No | >5 weeks | |
| FoxPro | S.Cal | $60 | | No | <20 hr | |
| Government Proposal/ Writing F100 | DC | | $950+exp. | No | 2-3 mos | F100 |
| HR Application Dev't | Remote clients | $72 | | No | | 20 years, CEBS |
| IBM 370/BAL/COBOL | Charlotte, NC | $50 | | Yes | 6 mos + | 30+ yrs |
| IEF Analyst, Senior | Travel | $60-88 | | Yes | | 3+ years exp. w. IEF |
| IEF Instructor | Travel | $70-105 | | Yes | | |
| IEF Programmer | Travel | $38-60 | | Yes | | <3 years exp. w. IEF |
| IEF Project Leader | Travel | $70-105 | | Yes | | Full Lifecycle experience |
| Lotus 1-2-3 | Boston | $100 | | No | <1 wk | Published Expert |
| Lotus 1-2-3 | Boston | | $800 | No | 6 mos | Published Expert |
| Lotus Notes/F100 | Charlotte, NC | $125 | | Yes | Sporadic | 3 yrs /Notes |
| Lotus Notes | NYC (on-site) | $80 | | Yes | | 30+ total |
| Lotus Notes | NYC | | 1500 | Yes | | |
| Mainframe Package Support | Italy | $100+car | | No | 2 yrs | |
| Management/Strategic/ Database | Travel | | $750-1000 | No | | Ex-MIS exec |
| Management/Strategic/ Software Dev't | Travel | | $1600-2000 | No | | Ex-CEO Software Company |

| Specialty | Location | Rate/hr | Rate/day | Brokered | Length | Experience |
|---|---|---|---|---|---|---|
| MAS/Acct Software | Hartford | $125 | | No | 40+ | CPA |
| MAS/Acct Software Support | Hartford | $80 | | No | 5-60/yr | CPA |
| Midrange/PC Programming | Austin (on-site) | $65 | $750+exp | No | | |
| MOTIF/Eiffel | Dayton, OH | $80 | | No | 1 yr | OOP Expert |
| MS Access Programming | Hartford | $80 | | No | | CPA |
| MSA/Mainframe Accounting Packages | Atlanta (home/on-site) | $35 | | Yes | 1 year | 16 years F100 |
| MSA | Remote clients | $60 | | No | Few hours | 16 years F100 |
| Network Engineering | DC | $90 | | No | Short term | 20 years, no CNE |
| Novell/Network Install/Support | Denver | $75 | | No | <8 hrs | |
| Novell/Network Install | Denver | $18-22 | | Yes | <8 hrs | |
| Novell/Network Install | Denver | $20-30 | | Yes | <8 hrs | |
| Novell/Network Support | Charlotte, NC | $65 | | | | |
| Novell Network Install/Support | Hartford | $100 | | No | | CPA |
| Oracle CASE/DBA | Travel | $65 | | No | 2+ yrs | |
| Oracle CASE Dev't | Travel | $56 | | No | 1000 hrs | |
| Oracle CASE Devt | Travel | $65 | | No | 300 hrs | |
| Oracle CASE | N. Cal | | $1000 | No | 9 hr days | Published Expert |
| Oracle CASE | Travel | | $1200+air | No | 9 hr days | Published Expert |
| PC Development | DC | $60-75 | | No | Long-term | |
| PC General | North Central IN | $50 | | No | | |
| PC Programming | Austin (home) | $50 | | No | | |
| PC Set Up/Support | | $75 | | No | <mo | |
| Reengineering, Insurance | Chicago | $150 | | No | <6 wks | MBA/CPA |
| Reengineering, Mfg | NJ | $80 | | No | 3 mos | MBA/CPA |
| SAS | | $50-60 | | No | 9 mo-2 yr | |
| Smalltalk | Boston | $75 | | No | 3 mo+ | 4 yrs |
| Smalltalk | New York | $75 | | No | 3 mo+ | 4 yrs/Wall St. |
| Smalltalk | Hartford | $35 | | Yes | 6 mo + | 3 yrs F100 Smalltalk Devt |

| Specialty | Location | Rate/hr | Rate/day | Brokered | Length | Experience |
|---|---|---|---|---|---|---|
| SQLWindows | NYC (on-site) | $95 | | No | 2 yrs | 18 years F100 |
| Strategy, Govt | DC | $100 | | No | <6 wks | MBA/CPA |
| Strategy, Insurance | NJ | $150 | | No | <6 mo | MBA/CPA |
| Strategy, Mfg | NY/LI | $125 | | No | <6 wks | MBA/CPA |
| Synon/AS/400 | LA | $55 | | | 3 mo | 6 yrs |
| System Programming IBM Mainframe | NY/NJ | $50 | | No | | |
| SystemProgramming IBM Mainframe | NY/NJ | $50 | | Yes | | |
| System Programming Mainframe | Travel | $50-75 | | Yes | | First contract |
| System Programming Tandem | SF | $45-55 | | Yes | | |
| System Programming Tandem | SF | $50-65 | | Yes | | Experienced |
| System Programming Tandem | SF | $75-100 | | Yes | | Top skills |
| System Programming VMS | NYC (on-site) | $75 | | No | 2days-18 mo | |
| Tandem/App Dev't | SF | $45-55 | | Yes | | |
| Train/Access Intro | | $15 | | Yes | | |
| Train/Access Dev't | NYC (on-site) | $95 | | | | MS Certified |
| Train/Lotus Notes | NYC (on-site) | | $1200 | | | |
| Train/Networking Advanced | Travel | | $1000 | | 1-4 wks | Ex-vendor engineer |
| Train/Networking Intro | Travel | | $650 | | 1-4 wks | Ex-vendor engineer |
| Train/Oracle CASE | Travel | | $1750+exp | | 5 days | Published Expert |
| Train/Visual Basic | NYC (on-site) | | $800 | Yes | 10 days/mo | 18 years F100 |
| Visual Basic | DC | $65 | | Yes | | |
| Visual Basic | LA | $30-35 | | Yes | 2-5 mos | |
| Visual Basic | NYC (on-site) | $75 | | No | 2 yrs | 18 years F100 |
| Visual Basic | Travel | $60 | | No | | |
| Visual C++ | LA | $45 | | Yes | 2-5 mos | |
| Windows Database Development | NYC (on-site) | $60 | | No | 8 mos | |

## WORKSHEET: Determine the "Going Rate"

1. If you offer programming as your main service, call up a selection of local consulting firms and ask them what hourly rate they would be willing to pay someone with your skills.

   Write the rate(s) you get here.......................$_____/hr

   Divide the above rate(s) by .65,
   Write the answer here.................................$_____/hr

   This is the rate a client would have to pay the consulting firm for your services

2. If you offer systems analysis, configuration, sales, or support, pose as a client and call up several competing consultants in your niche and region. Ask them what hourly rates they charge.

   Write the rate(s) you get this way here..........$_____/hr

3. Post queries asking for rate feedback on computer bulletin boards or Internet newsgroups. Remember to specify your location, specialty and clientele.
   Write the rate(s) you get this way here..........$_____/hr

4. Attend meetings of consultants and keep your ears open. If you hear of a rate that relates to your specialty, ask how long the assignment for which that rate was charged lasted.

   Write the rate(s) you hear this way here.........$_____/hr

5. Ask other consultants what they'd recommend as a rate for someone with your skills. (Don't ask directly what they earn. Most people will exaggerate in that situation.)

   Write the rate(s) you get this way here..........$_____/hr

6. Throw out any rates that are much higher or lower than the rest.

7. Average the rates you've come up with and write them here. This is the "going rate".....................................................$_____/hr

## WORKSHEET: Double-Check Your Rate Against the "Rule of Thumb"

1. Write down the Annual Salary of an Employee with your skills and write it here...........................................$_____/yr

   If you don't know this amount, you can estimate it by:

   - Looking at job advertisements in the Sunday classifieds.

   - Calling a local job placement firm that specializes in computer personnel and asking them what salary they could get you.

   - Finding the "Annual Salary Survey" issue of *Computerworld* or *Datamation* at any large college or city library and looking up your niche.

2. Divide the employee's annual salary by 1,000 and write the answer here................................................$_____/hr
   This is the *"rule of thumb"* hourly rate for your specialty.

3. Now compare this rate with the "going rate" you calculated above. The going rate should be close to the "rule of thumb" rate. If it is, you can feel safe use the "going rate" as your rate.

## GOTCHA!!

If your "rule of thumb" rate is significantly higher than your "going rate," you've got a problem. Either:

- Low consulting rates in your region may reflect lack of demand for consultants with your skills or—

- You may not have done enough research to ensure you have an accurate going rate.

## CHECK YOUR RATE AGAINST YOUR EXPENSES

Now that you've established a rate, you need to make sure that the rate you've come up with is high enough to cover your expenses and still leave you a profit. You'll do this by estimating your expenses and subtracting those expenses from what you hope to earn at your new rate.

Use the following list to estimate your annual business expenses. Do *not* count expenses that you'd be paying if you were not in business—like the cost of computers and software you'd buy for your own use at home, the cost of the commute to and from work each day, or the cost of a business suit you'd also need for a salaried job.

# WORKSHEET: Calculate Your Expenses

| ITEM | Annual Expense |
|------|----------------|
| | $ |
| **Office Expense** | |
| Office Supplies | |
| Stationary | |
| Postage | |
| Miscellaneous | |
| **Hardware and Software** | |
| Hardware bought for business | |
| Software bought for business | |
| **Networking/Professional Costs** | |
| Phone bills | |
| Travel to attend meetings | |
| Fees for local meetings | |
| Fees for courses/seminars | |
| Fees for professional societies | |
| Journals and magazines | |
| On-line services/email | |
| Professional books | |

| ITEM | Annual Expense |
|---|---|
| **Insurance/ Benefits Costs** | $ |
| General Liability Insurance | |
| Business Property Insurance | |
| Health Insurance | |
| Disability Insurance | |
| Retirement Plan | |
| | |
| **Costs of Doing Business** | |
| Registrations and permits | |
| Gas/tolls for local travel | |
| Parking | |
| Gifts to clients/referrers | |
| | |
| **Professional Services** | |
| Attorney | |
| Accountant | |
| Graphic Design/DTP | |
| | |
| **Other Business Expenses** | |

**TOTAL EXPENSES**       $_____

## WORKSHEET: Determine Your Net Income

1. Write your estimated total annual expenses
   here..................................................................$_____

2. If you are a contract programmer, divide this figure by
   1,500...............................................................$_____

   Otherwise, divide this figure by 1,000...............$_____/hr
   This is your *Expenses per Hour*

3. Write your Hourly Rate here............................$_____/hr

4. Deduct the expenses per hour
   from your hourly rate. ......................................$_____/hr
   this is your *Net Hourly Rate Before Taxes*

5. Multiply the net hourly rate by .70....................$_____/hr
   This is your estimated *Net Hourly Rate After Taxes*

6. If you are a contract programmer, multiply the net hourly rate
   after taxes by 1,500. Otherwise multiply it by
   1,000................................................................$_____
   This  is what you'd earn in after-tax income
   if you were to work an average number of
   consulting hours per year

7. Now, multiply your net hourly rate after taxes by
   750..................................................................$_____
   This is what you'd earn in a typical bad year

Are you happy with these numbers? Would they make it worth the hassle of running your own business?

If the answer is "yes," you've come up with a rate you can live with.

If the answer is "no," then you may not be able to make a living in your region at the kind of consulting you have in mind.

## BILLING EXTRAS

There are a number of situations consultants run into where it is not clear whether it is appropriate to bill clients for their time or for extraordinary expenses the consultant must incur.

There is no set way in which consultants handle these situations. You will need to think through how you will handle each of these issues before you quote a rate to a client.

The following list presents the most common situations in which such billing questions arise and the various methods consultants use to handle them. If you *do* decide to bill for any of these "extras," make sure your client is aware in advance that you will be charging for them.

### HOW DO YOU BILL FOR. . .

**Billing Item:** Initial meetings with clients before a contract is agreed upon.

**Options:**

- Bill for all time you spend with clients at your usual hourly rate.

- Bill for any time you spend after you give the client one free hour in which they may discuss their needs.

- Treat all time spent making a sale as marketing expense and provide it free—as long as the earnings from the project will justify the time you spend securing it.

> ## GOTCHA!!
>
> The single most common reason clients withhold payment is to protest the inclusion of an unexpected expense item on their bill.
>
>

**Billing Item:** Time spent on telephone calls in which the client asks for advice and/or software or hardware support.

### Options:

- Bill for time spent answering all support calls.

- Bill for all calls longer than some pre-defined time.

- Charge a monthly amount (payable in advance) for unlimited phone support.

- Provide free support to encourage clients to call and book new projects.

**Billing Item:** Lengthy long distance phone calls made to clients and to vendors on behalf of the client.

### Options:

- Bill for all long distance calls.

- Bill for long distance calls costing over some preset amount.

- Make sure your hourly rate is high enough to cover all long distance calls and provide them "free."

**Billing Item:** Hotel, airfare, car rental fees, and costs of meals when traveling out of town on behalf of a client.

### Options:

- Add to your usual rate, a fixed "per diem" travel allowance high enough to cover all travel expenses.

- Charge your usual rates. Have the client make all travel arrangements and pay for them.

- Charge a daily rate high enough to cover any travel expenses.

**Billing item:** The cost of hours spent on the plane and at the hotel while traveling out of town on behalf of a client.

### Options:

- Charge regular hourly rates for all time spent in traveling.

- Charge a daily or weekly rate, rather than an hourly rate for any assignment that involves travel.

- Charge only for time spent working for the client.

***Billing item:*** Time and money spent mastering bleeding edge technology on the client's behalf.

### *Options:*

- Charge your usual rate for all time you spend learning a new technology when there are no experts available who have already mastered the technology, or if the experts' rates are so high the client prefers to pay you to learn, or when a client prefers to work with you as a known quantity rather than bring in an unknown "expert."

- Accept a lower rate or, in some cases, work for free, to induce a client to give you a chance to work with a new technology if this training will make your services more valuable to other clients in the future.

## PAYMENT SCHEDULES

### Q: What is the biggest problem consultants have with billing?

**A:** Getting paid. Particularly in situations where payment doesn't occur until the project has been completed and delivered.

### Q: Why is waiting for payment until a project is completed such a bad idea?

**A:** Because once the project is complete and the software and hardware are installed on the client's site, he or she has little incentive to pay you.

### Q: Can't I repossess systems and software if my client doesn't pay me?

**A:** No. You can't repossess anything unless you have put specific legal wording into your contract that defines it as a time-payment contract and defines the conditions under which you can repossess. That wording is almost never found in computer consulting contracts. Without that wording, the hardware and software you deliver to clients may be theirs to keep even if they don't pay you.

### Q: Can't I sue if a client doesn't pay me?

**A:**. You can sue, but even when you have a good case against a deadbeat client, lawsuits for nonpayment are costly, time consuming, and often ineffective. This is particularly true when the client turns out not to have the money needed to pay you. In such cases you may get a legal judgment and still be unable to collect a cent.

## PAYMENT SCHEDULES THAT WORK

Your best defense against deadbeat clients is to negotiate a payment schedule into any contract you sign. The goal of such a schedule is to:

- Require proof that the client intends to pay.

- Give you income to sustain you through a long contract.

- Keep payments to a manageable size making it easier for clients to come up with the money to pay them.

- Allow you to bail out of a project *before* you sustain a huge loss if it becomes clear you are dealing with a deadbeat.

We'll discussing this topic further in Chapter Six when we discuss specific computer consulting contract clauses.

---

## HOW TO SCHEDULE PAYMENTS

### FIXED BID:

The traditional way to schedule payments in a fixed bid situation is to require that the client pay:

- Some percentage of the total fee (often 1/3) before the project starts.
- Some percentage at each of one or more mid-project checkpoints.
- The remainder when the project is complete.

If payment is not received within a stated period after these agreed upon milestones are achieved, work stops on the project.

### HOURLY RATE:

When billing on an hourly rate basis:

- Send out invoices on a regular schedule, either every two weeks or monthly.
- Specify in the contract how long a grace period the client has before payment is expected.
- Specify in the contract that if more than a preset number of invoices remain unpaid, work stops on the project.

## TAKING CREDIT CARDS

If you have decided to serve the home office/small business market or if you intend to sell software, books, or hardware through mail order you may want to consider applying for merchant status so that your clients and customers can purchase goods and services from you using their credit cards.

### Q: How do I become authorized to accept credit card payments?

**A:** If you have a retail business and good credit, you may be able to get merchant status—the ability to process credit card transactions—through your bank.

If you don't operate a storefront but work out of a home office, you will find it harder to get merchant status through your bank and will probably have to hunt around for a third party vendor who offers this service to small businesses like yours for a fee.

### Q: How do I begin the process of getting merchant status?

**A:** Call your local bank and ask them if they will give you merchant status. Even without a storefront, some banks may grant you merchant status if you open a secured account in their bank that contains enough money in it to cover the amounts you expect your clients to charge on credit cards. Other banks may simply refer you to third party vendor companies.

### Q: How much can I expect to pay for Merchant Status?

**A:** The deals available to businesses without storefronts generally include charges similar to what you see in the table of credit card processing fees you'll find on Page 107. There may be other fees as well. For example, a bank granting merchant status may require that you purchase a long-term CD from them in an amount of anywhere from $3,000-5,000. You'll need to talk to a vendor to determine the exact charges you'll have to pay.

### Q: So accepting credit card orders in the amount of $25,000 a year could cost me something like $1,760 or 7% of my sales?

**A:** That's right. You may want to do some serious thinking about whether the extra customers this will bring you is worth the expense. Corporate customers will want to establish credit accounts with you instead of using a credit card for business purchases. When business clients do use credit cards, they often use American Express corporate cards. So be sure that any third party vendor you hook up with can process AMEX transactions too, since not all can.

## Table 4. Credit Card Processing Expenses

| CHARGE | AMOUNT | EXPLANATION |
|---|---|---|
| Set up fee | $125-225 | Pays the commission of the salesperson selling you the service |
| Monthly statement fee | $5/mo | Charged whether or or not you make any transactions |
| Transaction fee | $.25-.33 | Charged for each charge you process |
| Rental of card Processing machine | $35-50/mo | Pays for the terminal that reads the customer's card and prints a receipt |
| Purchase of card Processing machine | $750 or $30-50/mo for 2 yrs | Alternative to rental |
| Processing software | $300-750 | Alternative to terminal if you process mail order transactions only |
| Percentage charge | 2-3% | Percentage on the total sale charged by the credit card company, plus another percentage or two of profit to the third party firm. It will be higher for transactions taken on the phone or by mail. |

**Q: As a computer consultant, do I have to accept credit cards?**

**A:** No. Many computer consultants do not.

## CUT RATES AND DISCOUNTS

It is a truism that everyone likes a bargain, but you should think long and hard before you cut your rates to attract more business. Cutting rates is often the first so-called "marketing" idea new consultants come up with. But if you have the skills it takes to be a successful computer consultant, charging a lower-than-market rate in and of itself rarely brings in new clients, and it may weaken your professional image.

Consider lowering your rates only if:

- You are charging a rate above the going rate for your specialty in your region and you are not able to find any work at that rate.

- You are not getting enough work at the rate you are charging to stay in business and could make a profit if you got more work at a lower rate.

- You have lost several contracts to other consultants who have the same skills and level of experience as you do, but who charge significantly less than you charge.

- A good client is willing to guarantee you a significant number of hours if you will discount your rate and you aren't likely to fill all those hours with work that pays at a higher rate.

- There's a job you really want to do that will let you learn something new and useful, and the rate for that job is not negotiable.

> ## GOTCHA!!
>
> The occupational hazard of computer consulting is WORKING FOR FREE.
>
> You should be the one to decide when to give your services away and when to sell them.
>
> Don't let clients or supposed friends manipulate you into feeling that the work that you do for them has no value.
>
>

## WHEN SHOULD YOU NOT DISCOUNT YOUR RATE?

Never discount your rate:

- When you're busy.

- When you are getting enough work at your high rate to tide you through the times when you don't find work.

- When you know for certain that your rate is the going rate for your skills in your region and know others who are currently earning that rate.

- When the discounted rate is too low to make working profitable.

## WHY RAISE YOUR RATE?

It's always hard to know when it's time to raise rates. If you're busy and have lots of happy clients, why rock the boat? But at the same time, if you could raise your rate and still keep those happy clients, you'd have that much more money to invest in training, or your retirement fund—or to cover the inevitable slow periods all consultants face.

Consider raising your rates when:

- You have had more than one client offering you more work than you can handle for at least six months.

- Most other consultants with skills similar to your own in your region are asking a higher rate than you are.

- Your credentials suggest that what you have to offer is a "premium service" and you want your rate to signal this to clients.

- Clients remark how cheap your rates are.

- You don't want to do a certain kind of project and are willing to use a high rate to discourage clients from asking for it—or to ensure that if you take on such a project, doing it is worth your while.

## HOW TO RAISE YOUR RATES

**Q:** *I've got several good clients I've worked for for several years, and I've always charged them the same rate. I'd like to raise my rate now but I'm not sure how to go about doing it without upsetting my clients.*

**A:** Give your clients some advance notice so that they can get used to the idea. Then, when you do announce a rate hike, set the proper tone. Don't be apologetic or suggest by your manner that you expect them to be upset. Simply thank them for their business, state that that the time has come to raise your rates, and describe your new rate structure.

When raising rates, some consultants offer steady clients the opportunity to continue a bit longer at their old rate in return for buying a guaranteed number of future hours. However, if you are busy and have not raised your rates in a while, it is not necessary to do this.

---

# GOTCHA!!

## Have I Got A Deal For You!

Never agree to develop a piece of software in return for a percentage of royalties from the future sale of that software. In 999 out of 1,000 cases, if you accept that kind of deal (as many neophyte consultants do) you'll never see a penny.

Clients who offer this kind of arrangement rarely if ever have any idea of what it takes to market a commercial software package and almost always propose these deals as a way of getting free software for their own use.

The few companies who do have a track record of successfully developing and marketing software products do not pay programmers royalties to develop software for them. They pay hourly rates or salaries and pay royalties to developers only when buying the rights to products that have already been developed and are proving themselves in the marketplace.

## Example 1. A Letter Announcing a Rate Increase

November 15, 1995


Dear Client,

It's been more than two years since I increased our rates, and I wish I could go two more. But unfortunately I can't. On January 3, 1996 I must increase our base rate from $55/hour to $65/hour. This is in line with what our colleagues and competitors charge locally and nationally.

There's good news, however. In the past two years we have built our programming library and software development utilities to the point where we are now about 25% more efficient than we were two years ago, resulting in projects that take less time to complete. The net result is that it may not cost you any more money than it did two years ago for the same size project.

[*Include the following when necessary:*
By special agreement, your current rate is a discounted $45 per hour. This will increase to $55 per hour instead of $65, maintaining roughly the same discount.]

If you would like, I can offer you a discount on future work if you prepay fifty-hour blocks of programming time at your current rate prior to the date when the rates will otherwise go up. This option will save you quite a bit of money if you will be needing our services in the future. Your rate increase would then be delayed until after you have used up your prepaid time. Your weekly invoices until then will reflect a credit balance.

Please phone me if I can help you estimate the hours required for a project. I appreciate your business, and am looking forward to working with you in the future.

Sincerly,

Copyright 1994 Rob Cosgrove. Used by permission.

# RATE CONTROVERSIES

### Should you bill one rate for one kind of work and another rate for another kind of work?

**NO:** Since clients are paying for your time, it is immaterial what kind of work you do in that time, so you should charge one rate for that time. Anything else raises ethical issues.

**YES:** Some kinds of work require much more effort than others. Some are more fun than others. Charging different rates for different kinds of work gives you a way of balancing these factors. You're being paid for both your time and your effort, so there's nothing unethical about charging different prices for different kinds of work—restaurants do it all the time.

### Should you charge all clients the same rate for the same work?

**YES:** If you don't, word will get out and you'll earn bad will. Plus, it may appear unethical or discriminatory to charge different rates to different clients.

**NO:** Huge corporations can afford to pay high rates—and expect to do so, while smaller businesses may only be able to afford discounted services. Plus, you may want to charge your old, steady customers your old, lower rate as a way of rewarding their loyalty while raising rates for new clients.

**Note:** If you are selling software products or books rather than pure services, there may be laws requiring you to offer the same discounts you give to one customer of a certain type to ALL customers of that type.

### Should you set a low rate to attract new clients?

**YES:** Work for as little as you can get by on if it gets you the contracts you need to build up a client list and get real-world experience.

**NO:** Low rates mark you as an amateur and attract low quality, cheapskate clients. High rates signal professionalism. If you can't find clients at a market rate for your skills, you probably aren't ready to start consulting.

# SOAP BOX

Fill in your responses in the following dialogue. Then practice delivering your answers out loud with a friend.

**Client:** How much do you charge for your services?

**You:**

**Client:** Would you be willing to do this project for a fixed price?

**You:**

**Client:** What can I do to get a discount on your rates?

**You:**

**Client:** Your rates seem kind of high to me.

**You:**

**Client:** Do you charge this amount to all your clients?

**You:**

**Client:** I'll pay you when the project is complete.

**You:**

**Client:** Do you take credit cards?

**You:**

## NOTES ON RATES

Use this page to jot down information you collect about rates:

# 4 HOW TO FIND CLIENTS

**CHAPTER OBJECTIVE**

**Master the marketing techniques that bring in new clients**

- Learn which marketing techniques work best for computer consultants
- Decide which ones are right for you
- Make the most of networking opportunities
- Discover how to run a cheap public relations campaign
- Raise your public profile by publishing
- Find clients through classes and seminars
- Cold call to jump-start an ailing practice

First the *bad news*: If you're looking for "Five Surefire Ways to Find New Clients Today," you're out of luck. The marketing techniques that work for computer consultants are slow-acting, long-term strategies that cannot be implemented instantly.

But the *good news* is that those long-term strategies do work. If you have the skills, credentials, and personality traits we discussed in Chapter One, the marketing techniques you'll find here will attract the clients you need to stay in business.

## GOTCHA!!

If you're starting out your practice with a client in hand, the **biggest** mistake you can make is to think you don't need to worry about marketing.

Failure to market while busy is the single most common reason for consulting failure. Most successful consultants report that they devote at least an hour every week to activities whose only purpose it to find them new clients.

The key is persistence. Marketing must be an ongoing conscious effort you pursue week in and week out. It may take six months or longer for these techniques to bear fruit, but if you persist, your efforts will pay off.

## DEVELOP A MARKETING MESSAGE

Before you can market, you must put considerable effort to isolating the message that will be the focus of your marketing efforts.

That's because in most marketing situations you will have fifteen seconds to get your point across. So it is vital that you know exactly what that point is going to be.

An effective marketing message should be simple, precise, and persuasive. It must connect with whatever it is that motivates clients to buy your kind of service, and get across why they should call you up and not another consultant.

You've already laid the groundwork for developing your marketing message with the worksheets you filled out in Chapter One. Now it's time to sharpen the focus of that message even more.

## WORKSHEET: Sharpen Your Marketing Message

*Use the following worksheet to help you find the most effective marketing message for your services.*

1. What do you think is the most important benefit you provide for clients?


2. What "pain" do clients experience that makes them willing to pay for your services?


3. What do you do for clients that will result in their earning more money than they paid you?


4. What would you like to hear a satisfied client say about your work?


5. When clients have praised you and compared your work to that of others, what have they said?


6. What is your clients' greatest business-related fear?


7. Which, among all the services you provide clients, is the one they believe they need most?

## UNDERSTANDING THE "Sharpen Your Marketing Message" WORKSHEET

Did you find it easy to fill in the worksheet on Page 117? Most new consultants don't. That's because they've learned to describe their job performance in the buzzword-laden catch phrases that pad out performance appraisals.

These phrases may make employees feel good about themselves but they sidestep the critical issue of what their real value might be to employers. After all, what employer is going to say, "We appreciate having you here because your salary is low, you do what we tell you, and you rarely call in sick."

Look through the following list of empty appraisal-style catch phrases. Did you use any of them when trying to list the benefits you provide clients?

- "I'm a team player"

- "I provide leadership"

- "I understand the needs of the organization"

- "I have excellent communications skills"

No one is going to rush to call you if this kind of vague blandness is all you can offer them.

Ask yourself, "Where does my client feel pain?" Then craft a marketing message that says, "I can make that pain go away." Here are some better examples of effective ways to describe what you do:

- "I write software that works the way it is supposed to and is cheap to maintain."

- "I understand your business, so I can provide software that does the tasks you need done, the way you expect them to be done."

- "I can keep your network up and running so that you can worry about more important things."

- "I know how devastating it would be if you lost your company's data and I know how to prevent that from happening."

- "I can show you how to use the information you already have on your database to generate more sales and locate new customers."

# MARKETING PRINCIPLES FOR CONSULTANTS

### PRINCIPLE #1: YOUR CLIENTS ARE ALREADY OUT THERE

The point of all your marketing efforts will to connect with people who already know they need the services you offer. These people exist. You do not need to create them. You're looking to be a match maker, *not* to make converts.

### PRINCIPLE #2: YOU NEED TO UNDERSTAND WHAT REALLY MOTIVATES YOUR CLIENTS

Clients don't wake up thinking, "Today I'm going to spend money on high-quality, new technology!" Clients spend money only when they're forced to—when that's what it takes to make a major headache go away, or to end up with *more* cash in their pockets.

If you can convince a client that you know what his or her headache is and that you *can* make it go away—or if you can convince them that you know where their money comes from and can make more of it appear, you'll make the sale. It's as simple as that.

### PRINCIPLE #3: MARKETING TAKES TIME

Marketing is a slow, long-term process, whose effects increase exponentially with time. You have to market faithfully and continuously for at least six months before you can expect your efforts to begin to bear fruit.

### PRINCIPLE #4: NO ONE HIRES A HUNGRY CONSULTANT

Marketing is toughest when you desperately need work. So the best time to market is when you're up to your ears in clients—or a year or two before you launch your consulting career.

If you do have to market when you're hungry, avoid making direct appeals for work. Most people feel uncomfortable or even guilty when confronted with that kind of request. So instead of asking for work, simply ask for a referral. Instead of suggesting that you are desperate to find new clients, just say you're eager to find interesting new projects to work on and would appreciate it if acquaintances would mention you to their friends.

### PRINCIPLE #5:  IT ISN'T MARKETING UNLESS IT BRINGS IN PAYING CLIENTS

If after six months your marketing efforts haven't resulted in phone calls from people willing to pay you money for your services, reconsider your marketing strategies.

Have you been giving away services to people who could not afford to pay for those same services, or spending your marketing time designing impressive business cards? You may call these kinds of activities "marketing" but they aren't. If your marketing activities are not putting you or your ideas in front of people who buy consulting services, they aren't true marketing activities.

### PRINCIPLE #6:  COMPUTERS ARE LOGICAL, PEOPLE ARE NOT

Never assume other people will make rational decisions. They won't. Nor can you control everything merely by thinking it through. After you've done all your planning and figuring, leave some room for the unpredictable. Though you can achieve a great deal through proper planning, you may also achieve as much by being at the right place at the right time—something you cannot control.

### PRINCIPLE #7:  THIS IS SUPPOSED TO BE FUN

Never follow any business "strategy" or advice that takes the fun out of what you do for a living. The consultants who last in this business are those who love their work.

---

## SOAP BOX

### "What's In It For You!"

Give a two-minute speech in which you describe to a client the benefits they'll get from the services you offer.

Back up your statements by giving concrete examples drawn from work you've done for previous clients or for an old employer.

## THE POWER OF WORD OF MOUTH

**Q: I've heard that most consultants find their clients through "word of mouth." What exactly is "word of mouth?"**

**A:** "Word of mouth" refers to recommendations and referrals you get from other people, especially past clients. It is so important because most clients are wary of hiring an unknown consultant and prefer to hire someone who comes recommended by a friend or associate. This is why advertising does little to attract consulting clients and why the ultimate goal of all your marketing efforts should be to get word of mouth working for you.

**Q: But this sounds like a classic Catch-22 situation. I'm just starting out, so how can I get referrals from satisfied clients when I don't have clients?**

**A:** This is a classic Catch-22 situation, and presents a serious challenge to all new consultants. However, when you're just starting out you should be able to generate enough word of mouth referrals from friends, neighbors, and people you have worked with in the past to get a client stream started.

**Q: I still don't like the idea of sitting around waiting for other people to send me clients. I want to find them myself.**

**A:** It is a mistake to assume that your role in generating word of mouth is a passive one. You can—and must—do a great deal to generate those word of mouth referrals. Doing just that is the intent of most of the marketing activities that you'll read about in the following pages.

## WHICH MARKETING TECHNIQUE IS FOR YOU?

There are quite a few reliable marketing techniques available to computer consultants. But few consultants have the time or energy to try out more than a few of them. That makes it essential that you determine which techniques are most likely to pay off for the kind of consulting you do.

Because computer consultants pursue such a variety of niches, the techniques that work well for people in one niche may fall short when used by people who serve a different clientele. Then too, some marketing techniques demand special talents, while others require certain personality traits. Use the table on Page 122 to determine which techniques are the most likely to pay off for you.

## Table 5. Marketing Strategy by Niche

| CONTRACT PROGRAMMER | |
|---|---|
| Best Strategy | Cultivate contacts with past coworkers and bosses. |
| Second Best Strategy | Participate in technically-oriented networking events that involve face-to-face meetings with other contractors and with managers who use the technology in which you are expert. |
| Worth Trying | Network with established consultants who may refer you their overflow work. Contact brokers and consulting firms who place consultants on 1099 and hourly consulting projects. Check out the ads in classified sections in specialty programming magazines and large on-line services like Compuserve. |
| Worthless | Mass mailings, Yellow Pages and newspaper advertising, fee-charging directories of consultants, fee-charging referral services. |
| Sample Networking Locales | Monthly meetings of the DB2 Users Group, OS/2 Users Group, Data Processing Managers Association, or Independent Computer Consultants Association. |
| Marketing Materials Needed | Business card. Résumé. |

| STOREFRONT RESELLER | |
|---|---|
| Best Strategy | Yellow pages ads, repeating ads in newspapers and local business periodicals, networking at business functions. |
| Worth Thinking About | Coupon or special offer mailings to carefully selected lists. |
| Worthless | Fee-charging directories. Newspaper advertising supplement sections. |
| Sample Networking Locales | Local computer user groups, Chamber of Commerce, civic organizations, public school fundraising events. |
| Marketing Materials Needed | Professionally designed ads and flyers, business cards, brochures. |

## VAR/RESELLER No Storefront

| | |
|---|---|
| Best Strategy | Actively participate in business organizations and civic groups that attract your target client. |
| Second Best Strategy | Teach classes and give lectures on problem solving themes to groups that contain your target client. |
| Worth Trying | Do-it-yourself PR, cold calling, newsletters targeting past acquaintances and customers, carefully chosen vendor consultant programs. |
| Worthless | Mass mailings, newspaper and Yellow Pages ads—except in very small towns. Independent sales reps, unless you have a staff of five or more full time employees. |
| Sample Networking Locales | Chamber of Commerce meetings, Specialty software Users Group Meetings, Civic Center Business Computer Show. |
| Marketing Materials Needed | Business card. Brochure—but only if you have something impressive to put on it. Client list. |

## CUSTOM SOFTWARE DEVELOPER

| | |
|---|---|
| Best Strategy | Aggressively maintain contacts with business people, past clients, previous employers, coworkers, and other consultants in the area in which you specialize. |
| Second Best Strategy | Write problem-solving articles for trade publications read by your target client. |
| Worth Trying | Teach technical courses on your area of expertise through a large, well-respected seminar house. Cold calling. Carefully selected vendor consultant programs. Do-it-yourself PR. |
| Worthless | Mass mailings, fee-paid consultant directories. Independent sales reps, unless you have a staff of five or more employees. |
| Sample Networking Locale | Compuserve Forums that support the software platform you work on. Annual conventions of managers who use the kinds of specialty software and hardware you sell. Software Development '9x conventions. |
| Marketing Materials Needed | Business card. Client list. Clips of any publications. |

## MIS MANAGEMENT CONSULTANT

| | |
|---|---|
| Best Strategy | Publish books and articles in the trade press that define you as the expert in a carefully selected niche. |
| Second Best Strategy | Use every opportunity to speak before groups of managers and executives. |
| Worth Trying | Mail custom or canned newsletters to a carefully chosen list. Hook up with a large seminar house and tour the country teaching courses on topics of current management interest, do-it-yourself PR. |
| Worthless | Advertising, mass mailings, cold calling. Consultant directories. Referral lines. |
| Sample Networking Locale | Meetings of DPMA, SIM, ACM, IEEE, and other professional groups that attract executives who buy high level consulting services. |
| Marketing Materials Needed | Business card. Stationary. Client list. Newsletter. Brochure. |

### Q: I notice that you list mass mailings as being worthless for all consultants. What's wrong with mass mailings?

**A:** They don't work. Mass mailings are good for selling impulse items like books or specialty products not available in retail stores. But even for those items a typical response rate is .005. That means you can expect five sales for every thousand pieces of mail. But since people rarely buy *personal services* in response to mailings from strangers, the response rate to a mailing for your consulting services is likely to be .000–i.e., no response at all.

### Q: What about mass mailings to people I already know?

**A:** Mailings to friends and business acquaintances help remind people that you are in business and can be an important part of your ongoing marketing strategy. However, to be effective, the letter you send must not look or sound like a mass mailing. And even the best of mailings is not likely to bring in immediate work. If you are hunting for leads, a brief phone call to an acquaintance that touches base and asks, "What's new?" is more likely to be effective.

## Q: Why don't you recommend using an independent sales rep?

**A:** No single independent consultant bills enough to make it worthwhile for a good sales rep to represent them. Sales reps who have the skills and technical knowledge it takes to sell consulting services can always make much better money selling for a large consulting house. So almost the only way a lone consultant can draw on the talents of a capable sales rep is to work with a broker or a large consulting firm.

## Q: What's wrong with buying display ads in the Yellow Pages?

Yellow Pages ads usually generate calls from copier salespeople, coffee services, and insurance agents, not paying clients. They may also attract home computer users looking for free advice. The only consultants who report getting value from such ads are those who own retail stores and a few who practice in rural areas. To determine if your community is one where such an ad might bring in clients, see if there are lots of local CPAs running display ads in your Yellow Pages. If there are, the ads may be effective. Otherwise, stick with the one line Yellow Pages entry that is automatically generated when you install a business phone.

## MARKETER: KNOW THYSELF!

The most powerful marketing technique in the world isn't going to work if it requires you to do things you hate. So whatever niche you are in, you must make sure that you choose marketing techniques that are compatible with your personality. Refer to the table on Page 126 to see which techniques match your personality.

**Table 6. Marketing Techniques And The Personalities That Go With Them**

| NETWORKING WITH TECHNICAL PEOPLE | |
|---|---|
| WHAT'S INVOLVED | Talking about the details of solving hardware and software problems. |
| WHO YOU GET TO HANG OUT WITH | Other consultants, technically savvy clients and managers. |
| SKILLS REQUIRED | Technical wizard, good at "tech talk." |
| PERSONALITY TYPE | Obsessed with technology. May be shy, but shyness evaporates when a stranger describes an IRQ conflict. Reads *PC Magazine* for relaxation. |

| NETWORKING WITH BUSINESS PEOPLE | |
|---|---|
| WHAT'S INVOLVED | Participation in civic events and professional organizations. |
| WHO YOU GET TO HANG OUT WITH | Business people, executives. |
| SKILLS REQUIRED | Ability to say the word "proactive" without giggling. Ability to fit in with the personality style that prevails in local community. Comfortable speaking to strangers of all types. Tactful. Aware of politics. Responsible. Willing to volunteer to do the unglamorous jobs others don't want to do. |
| PERSONALITY TYPE | Enjoys meetings, has natural leadership abilities. |

| DO-IT-YOURSELF PR | |
|---|---|
| WHAT'S INVOLVED | Writing press releases and talking with journalists. |
| WHO YOU GET TO HANG OUT WITH | Yourself. Underpaid editors, journalists and freelancers. |
| SKILLS REQUIRED | Extremely good writing skills. Good analytic abilities. Good phone skills. Innate sense for what constitutes a new slant on old material. |
| PERSONALITY TYPE | Comfortable promoting self, but knows the difference between bragging and advertising. |

| LECTURING AND TEACHING | |
|---|---|
| WHAT'S INVOLVED | Teaching groups of potential clients. |
| WHO YOU GET TO HANG OUT WITH | People who look up to you as an expert. |
| SKILLS REQUIRED | Comfortable speaking before groups. Able to explain complex topics clearly. A very good sense of humor. Able to make other people feel good about themselves while explaining complex topics. |
| PERSONALITY TYPE | Outgoing, theatrical, comfortable controlling groups. |

| WRITING FOR THE BUSINESS AND PROFESSIONAL PRESS | |
|---|---|
| WHAT'S INVOLVED | Writing books and articles in your area of expertise. |
| WHO YOU GET TO HANG OUT WITH | Editors, other writers on-line, people you interview for your books and articles, but mostly yourself. |
| SKILLS REQUIRED | Adequate writing skills (not necessarily as good as what it takes to do PR.) |
| PERSONALITY TYPE | Can meet deadlines. Enjoys writing. Enjoys lecturing, since publishing articles usually leads to being invited to speak publicly. |

| MAILING A REGULAR NEWSLETTER | |
|---|---|
| WHAT'S INVOLVED | Putting something in the mail on a regular basis. Managing a mailing list. |
| WHO YOU GET TO HANG OUT WITH | Yourself. Writers you meet on-line. People you interview. |
| SKILLS REQUIRED | If writing the newsletter yourself, very good writing and desktop publishing skills. Understanding of how to work with mailing lists. |
| PERSONALITY TYPE | Doesn't mind being tied to a schedule. |

## PUT YOUR MARKETING PLAN INTO ACTION

Now that we've surveyed the marketing techniques available to you, we'll look at how you practice these techniques. We'll start out discussing networking since it is the single most important marketing technique used by all computer consultants.

## NETWORKING

The term "Networking" refers to all the activities you pursue that keep up existing connections with peers, clients, and other business associates and put you into situations where you can meet new ones. If this sounds simple—even simplistic—that's because it is. Most of us network unconsciously every day of our lives.

However, networking may present a challenge to super-techie computer consultants whose strength lies in their technical expertise, who may have been attracted to computers precisely because they have shy, introverted personalities. Such people often feel aversion at the thought of putting themselves into situations where the point is "merely" casual talk and socializing and may feel shy about calling up old acquaintances to reinforce friendships for business reasons.

If that's your situation, concentrate on finding networking venues that feature people you respect discussing subjects that interest you. You market most effectively when you are being yourself, doing what you love to do, and expressing genuine interest in the people you are interacting with. Networking doesn't have to be a chore and you don't have to act like a jerk to boost your business.

### SOAP BOX

Practice answering the question:

#### "So, What Do You Do?"

End your reply with a question that gets the person with whom you are speaking talking about themselves.

## HOW TO IMPROVE YOUR WORD OF MOUTH

Here's how to improve the word of mouth about your business:

1. Ask satisfied clients to pass your name on to anyone who might be able to use your services.

2. Tell everyone you come across in daily life what kind of work you do and mention that you are looking for consulting opportunities.

3. Participate in civic functions and volunteer for projects that bring you into contact with other business people as a "doer."

4. Lecture on your area of expertise to any group who will listen. As part of your presentation, briefly describe what you do and the kinds of projects you are looking for.

5. Send out press releases about your business with the goal of placing articles about your business in the local business news.

6. Remember that every local business community, no matter how large, is made up of hundreds of people each of whom knows dozens of other people, all of whom gossip constantly. Never say anything to anyone you wouldn't want to see on the front page of the newspaper—and *do* talk up the things you would like to have get around.

## HOW TO NETWORK WITHOUT BEING A JERK
### A Garland Of "Do's" And "Don'ts"

**DON'T**—Bother with events advertised as "networking opportunities." These attract the desperate and shysters looking to fleece them.

**DO**—Network at events that have a real agenda–one that interests you and the people you would like to work for.

**DON'T**—Forget that everyone you meet anywhere may know someone who could turn into a client.

**DO**—Carry your business cards with you always in case someone wants to know how to get in touch with you.

**DON'T**—Ask for work at a networking event.

**DO**—Let people know what your specialty is.

**DON'T**—Brag.

**DO**—Cite pertinent anecdotes that demonstrate your professionalism.

**DON'T**—Make yourself your main topic of conversation.

**DO**—Ask people lots of questions about their businesses.

**DON'T**—Get into deep time-consuming conversations about technical problems at business events.

**DO**—Offer to call or mail follow-up information if someone has a technical problem they'd like to discuss with you further.

**DON'T**—Volunteer to do a job unless you are sure you can follow through.

**DO**—Share referrals and useful information with others.

**DON'T**—Force your card on someone in a social situation unless they've expressed interest in speaking with you again.

**DO**—Write notes on the backs of business cards others hand you to remind yourself who they are and what you discussed with them.

**DON'T**—Assume that another person shares your political beliefs or prejudices. You are more likely to offend someone than make a connection with them by bringing up controversial topics.

**DO**—Treat everyone you meet with the same friendliness and respect you'd reserve for a major client and don't jump to conclusions about who can help your business and who is a waste of time.

## GET NOTICED

Networking with others is great way to get known in any business or professional community, but to really supercharge your efforts you need to *put yourself in front of people.*

You can do this by:

↗ Giving talks at conventions, monthly meetings of civic groups, and annual conventions of potential clients. Focus your talks on how to solve problems common to your target clientele.

↗ Teaching courses through college extension services, high school adult education services, and professional groups. The most effective classes are those in specialized topics likely to attract your target client.

↗ Volunteering for activities sponsored by civic groups, public schools, scouts, sports leagues and charities.

↗ Taking a leadership role in trade groups that serve your industry or profession.

↗ Presenting at trade shows that cater to your peers and clients.

## CULTIVATE YOUR EXISTING CONTACTS

Your best source of future work is the people you already know, particularly those who have worked with you professionally. Put an extra effort into maintaining these contacts and you will generate leads to the jobs you need.

Here are some ways to keep your network of existing contacts alive and producing:

• Send out letters to old business acquaintances once or twice a year letting them know what you are doing.

• Don't brag, but do mention any interesting projects you are working on to get across the idea that you have a flourishing consulting career.

• Remember that you make your best impression when you are busy so be sure to contact people then.

• When you hear that an acquaintance has gotten a promotion, made a job change, or won an award, write or call to congratulate them.

• Send out a newsletter to past clients and other acquaintances who are in a position to buy your services.

- Send good clients advertising premiums—calendars, note pads, or mouse pads with your company name on them.

- Send "Thank You" gifts to anyone who has sent you work or useful referrals. Food gift baskets are always a good choice.

- Take out to lunch other consultants who could send you referrals.

- Lunch with old coworkers every few months to catch up on who's doing what and to remind them of what you're doing now.

Example 2 on Page 133 suggests the kind of letter you would use to keep up your connection with an old coworker.

## NETWORK WITH OTHER CONSULTANTS

Networking with other consultants can be as productive or even more productive than networking with potential clients.

Why?

- Because overbooked consultants may refer you their overflow clients.

- Because consultants in other niches may refer you clients.

- Because consultants running large projects may ask you to subcontract.

- Because other consultants are usually the first to hear about new projects staffing up.

> ## GOTCHA!!
> ### FEAST OR FAMINE
> Consultants report they are either overwhelmed with work or have none all. After a long dry spell your marketing efforts may bring in more work than you can handle. Plan for this contingency by establishing relationships with other consultants to whom you can refer **your** overflow.
>
>

But the only way you will *get* work from other consultants, is if you *give* work to other consultants, or offer them technical help or back-up. No one is going to go out of their way to help you until you've established yourself as someone deserving of help.

## Example 2.  Keep-in-Touch Letter

```
                        Ozgood Petrie
                     Agency Systems, Inc.
                     1234 Fernwood Road
                     Anytown, US   01234




January 24, 1996


Jeff Stamper
Vice President
Management Information Services
Monopoly Insurance Company
Megapolis, CT   06789

Dear Jeff,

I just saw the announcement in Computerworld of your recent promotion to
Vice President.  They couldn't have made a better choice!  Please accept my
hearty congratulations on your well-earned success.

We've been extremely busy here at Agency Systems trying to keep up with the
demand for our custom PowerBuilder agency systems.  We'll be rolling out
three new installations this spring in three different cities—and we're
almost done with the specs for a fourth.

It's quite a change from the days when we used to stay up all night running
production parallels on that old 158, isn't it?

I look forward to seeing you at the FLMI convention.  Until then, best
wishes to you and yours.

Sincerely,


Ozzy
```

### CO-MARKETING

**Q: I notice you don't recommend forming a marketing consortium with other consultants. Why not?**

**A:** Forming a consultant consortium to share marketing expenses is one of those great ideas that never seems to work out in practice. Though many new consultants inquire about such consortia, I have yet to hear of a single one that lasted more than a year. Good consultants rarely need that kind of marketing help so fledgling consortia may end up attracting consultants who need marketing help because they don't have the skills it takes to succeed.

## NEWSPAPER ADVERTISING

**Q: Is advertising in newspapers or magazines worthwhile?**

**A:** Newspaper advertising is worthwhile only if you have the patience—and budget—to advertise steadily for six months or more. Newspaper advertising also makes sense only if a large percentage of the publication's readers fit the profile of your target client.

**Q: How can I tell if my clients will respond to ads?**

**A:** Call others who advertise services similar to yours—but not competing with yours—in the publication. Ask them how well their ads pulled.

**Q: I've heard that if you see an ad repeated in a publication over several months it is a sign that it is bringing in business.**

**A:** This may be true, but many publications offer big discounts to advertisers who contract to repeat their ads for six months. So you may see repeating ads that are not, in fact, bringing in business.

# How To Get an Article Written About Your Business

- Write out the primary selling message you'd like to get across.

  *Example:* "The systems I sell cut staffing needs in half."

- Next list achievements that back up this message.

  *Example:* "Acme Insurance Agency is getting their quotes into the mail twice as fast with half the staff after installing my software."

- Consider which publications would be the best place for an article: A computer trade paper like *Computerworld*? A specialty magazine like *Insurance Agency Weekly*? The business section of the local newspaper?

- Read a few issues of the publications you are considering. Look for stories about businesses like yours. What kinds of themes do they highlight?

- Write a headline in the style of your target publication. In your headline, emphasize a benefit your client will want for themselves:

  *Example:* "Half the Staff Does Twice the Work."

  Or highlight a human interest angle:

  *Example:* "Internet Expert Finds Missing Girl in Mongolia."

- Write a one-page press release that gives information to back up your headline. Use the guidelines you'll find on Page 136. Use a style as close as possible to that of the publication you are targeting.

- Address your release by name to the editor who is responsible for the section where feature stories about businesses like yours appear.

- Write out a list of supplementary facts you were not able to fit into the release. If an editor calls you for more information, use this list to give them more facts and ideas for an article.

- If you get written about, drop the editor a "Thank You" note.

- Keep up your relationships with editors by passing them any newsworthy tips you encounter—not just ones about your business.

- Don't send a blizzard of press releases to a single publication. Go for quality instead. One release every few months is enough for any publication.

- You can send out the same release to several publications. The resulting articles will usually end up quite different from each other as each editor is likely to find his or her own angle.

## HOW TO FORMAT A PRESS RELEASE

- At the top write "FOR IMMEDIATE RELEASE."

- If you do not want the story to appear before a certain date, write instead "FOR RELEASE MM/DD/YY".

- Follow this with a block of single-spaced contact information. Remember to include your name, your title if you use one, your business address, phone, and fax number, and any on-line mailbox you check daily.

- Begin your release with a brief informative headline that will catch a reader's interest.

- Double space the text of the release.

- Remember to answer the five "W's"—"Who," "What," "When," "Where," and "Why" if you are trying to generate a news story.

- Put a hook in the first paragraph if you are trying to generate a feature. A hook is a twenty-five word phrase that pulled out of the article and put on a magazine cover would make someone want to read the story.

- Keep the length of the text of your release to two pages or less.

- End with "###" or "-end-".

### HOW TO MAKE SURE THE EDITOR RUNS YOUR RELEASE

Editors get hundreds if not thousands of press releases. So keep the following points in mind if you want to keep yours out of the trash:

↗ Specialty publications are much more likely to run your release than mainstream magazines and often more effective for reaching a clearly defined specialty audience.

↗ Editors are always looking for stories that will entertain or inform their readership. Try to send them releases that can be turned into a feature article—ones with a strong hook that will interest their readers.

↗ Editors love it when you send them a release that can be used as an article without being rewritten.

↗ Editors love a local angle: If they can't find "Man bites dog," they'll usually settle for "Area dog bites man."

↗ Editors—even those who write about business, computers, and technology—rarely know much about these subjects. Never assume technical expertise in an editor and spell out any complex technical concepts essential for understanding your news story.

↗ Include names and contact information wherever possible when mentioning other businesses or professionals.

> ## GOTCHA!!
>
> Never chat freely when an editor calls. Anything you say may end up in the article—out of context and sounding far dumber than it did when you said it.
>
> Stick to a written agenda. If you can't answer a question immediately, say, "Let me get back to you on that" and do—after you've crafted an answer you'd feel comfortable seeing in print.
>
> Avoid mentioning any business failure unless it is absolutely necessary that it be there to add poignancy to a subsequent huge success.
>
>

## Example 3. This Press Release Generated Three Feature Articles

FOR IMMEDIATE RELEASE

Contact: Janet Ruhl
Ruhl Computer Services
P.O. Box 171
Leverett, MA    01054
(413) 548-9948

LOCAL AUTHOR TEACHES CONSULTING—THE SURVIVAL SKILL OF THE 90s.

Becoming a consultant used to be one of many career options open to professionals. But in today's climate of nonstop downsizing many professionals find that consulting is no longer an option but is the only method left to them of continuing their careers.

In her recently published book, THE COMPUTER CONSULTANT'S GUIDE (John Wiley, 1994, ISBN 0-471-59661-2) author Janet Ruhl makes it clear that consulting is not a quickie solution to being laid off and that the life of a consultant is far from being the wish fulfillment fantasy of "being your own boss."    Drawing on material provided by over 200 working consultants Ruhl paints a down-to-earth portrait of what real consultants do, how they do it, and what it takes for newcomers to break in.

"Ideally, the time to start preparing for a consulting career is while you are in your last year in college," says Ruhl. "The entry level job you take may do more to define your subsequent niche than any future work decision you may make." Ruhl also points out that the best time to begin marketing your consulting skills is while you have a job that you enjoy, when you are more likely to project your enthusiasm and competence to those you meet in professional situations and when you are likely to have more networking opportunities than you will when you go off on your own.

"Consulting can be a wonderful way of life, providing an ideal blend of income and free time, but achieving that state requires that you put a lot of effort into understanding how the business works," Ruhl explains. "And the best people to learn this from are other working consultants."

Ruhl herself interacts with other consultants on CompuServe's COMPUTER CONSULTANT'S FORUM, where she has been a staff member since 1990. The forum, an international clearinghouse for consulting tips, has attracted over 35,000 visitors this year. Visitors post questions about a wide range of business problems, from clients who won't pay for work already completed to what to do about romance on the job. Their queries are answered by other forum visitors or by the forum's staff of resident experts which include, besides Ruhl, an attorney, a CPA, and several successful consultants active in a variety of niches.

Ruhl will be offering a seminar, "Getting Started in Consulting" on November 5, at the University of Massachusetts Campus Center. For more information call 413 548-9948.


BACKGROUND:

Janet Ruhl's other books include THE PROGRAMMER'S SURVIVAL GUIDE: Career Strategies for Computer Professionals (Prentice Hall, 1989) and THE WRITER'S TOOLBOX: Buying and Using a Computer for the Literary Life (Prentice Hall, 1990).

###

## GIVE TALKS

The best way to give potential clients a "free sample" of your abilities is to give them a talk. Business and civic groups are always looking for new speakers to address their monthly meetings. So don't be shy about calling up local organizations and suggesting a topic you'd be willing to talk about.

If you aren't used to public speaking, start small and work your way up so you have time to develop confidence and hone your speaking technique. An ideal place to practice is a Special Interest Group (SIG) meeting of your local computer users group. Choose a topic you feel comfortable with and sign up for a twenty minute presentation.

Tape your speech and listen to it at home. What could you have improved? Note in particular how quickly you talk and how interesting your voice sounds. If you identify any serious problems with your delivery, look into taking a formal class in public speaking. or join a local Toastmaster's Club. If it is the quality of your voice itself that bothers you, contact a local voice teacher for some lessons.

If you speak well, people who attend your talks may invite you to speak elsewhere. Accept any invitation that exposes you to potential clients. Just make sure that the topics you speak on are ones that demonstrate your talents and encourage potential clients to think of you as an expert.

### WHAT IS A "PROBLEM SOLVER?"

The most effective speech or article you can write is what editors call "a problem solver." These are topics that discuss fears or problems common to your audience and offer solutions to them.

In practice, you may often find it useful to invent a problem to capture your audience's interest when discussing any topic. For example, rather than title a speech, "Software Usage Measurement Tools" you could recast it as a problem solver called, "Don't Get Fired for Buying Useless Software." This particular problem solver would focus on how data collected by software measurement tools might persuade management that the company is getting measurable value from their software—and the help protect the careers of managers who invested in that software.

## HOW TO IMPROVE YOUR VISIBILITY WITH PUBLIC SPEAKING

☑ *Send out press releases four weeks before the event to local newspapers and relevant business publications.*

> *Describe both the topic of your speech and your credential in the press release.*

> *Include a telephone number where you can be reached for more information.*

> *Write the release in a way that encourages an editor to interview you for a feature article.*

☑ *Send an announcement of your talk three weeks in advance to any local newspaper that runs a "local business events" calendar.*

☑ *Make sure that people who phone you get the information they need.*

> *Update your answering machine message to include information about your talk.*

> *Be sure to get complete contact information from all callers.*

> *Ask callers about themselves and their businesses and use this information to expand your network.*

☑ *Several weeks before your talk mail letters to business friends and acquaintances informing them about it.*

☑ *Make sure you have enough business cards and other marketing materials to handle the expected demand at your talk. If you don't, get more printed up.*

☑ *Announce your talk on computer bulletin boards.*

☑ *When people speak with you after your talk, ask for their business cards and note on the back of each card where you met them and any relevant topics of conversation you shared. Add these people to any mailing lists you maintain for newsletters or update letters.*

☑ *When people ask for more information about something cited in your talk, ask for their cards and offer to send them additional information. After you send it, phone them and ask if they have further questions now that they've seen the material.*

☑ *When people ask if you'd be interesting in doing some consulting for them, don't try to set something up on the spot. Just make an appointment for a meeting in which you can discuss their requirements further.*

## MARKET THROUGH CLASSES AND SEMINARS

Teaching is a good way to bring yourself to the attention of clients, but only if you teach courses that attract your target clientele. For example, if you were trying to sell management consulting services to executives, you would want to teach a course like "Business Process Reengineering," rather than an introductory "Meet the Computer" course. If you were trying to sell computer systems to local retailers, a non-credit junior college course entitled "Accounting Systems for Retail Businesses" might be ideal.

**Q: If I teach business people courses that let them "do it themselves" how will I end up getting business?**

**A:** People often sign up for seminars and classes on technical topics hoping to become experts but conclude after taking the course that they need a real expert to help them. As the teacher of the course, you are the obvious choice for that "expert."

For this reason, many seminar teachers make it a practice to call up attendees several weeks after a seminar is over. They inquire how they are doing with the new technology and to ask whether they have further questions now that they've taken the technology back to the workplace. These calls often result in consulting assignments.

### SOAP BOX

Come up with of three "problem solver" topics that let you show off your expertise. Pick one and turn it into a brief talk using the following six steps:

1. Describe the problem in 25 words or less.

2. Give a concrete example of what happens when the problem is *not* solved.

3. Describe the *usual* way of solving it, citing weaknesses in this solution.

4. Describe the solution you'd recommend which draws on your specialized knowledge of some tool, procedure, or technique.

5. List two or three facts or anecdotes to back up each argument you make.

## Q: How do I get a job teaching a class at a college or other educational institution?

**A:** Your best bet is to offer to teach a noncredit course through an institution's "continuing education," "extension," or "adult education" branch. No degree or other academic qualification is needed. All you need is a credential that suggests you know your material.

Before proposing a course, send off for catalogs from local institutions that offer non-credit courses and study them to see if what you have in mind would fit in with their other course offerings. These catalogs often include a form you can use to propose a course of your own. If you don't find such a form, call the director of the extension service and ask for information on how to propose a course. Remember that it will take anywhere from a few months to a year until your course gets scheduled, so don't propose anything too trendy or time-dependent.

## Q: How long does the class I offer have to be?

**A:** Many extension classes take only a single Saturday morning or a few weekday evenings. This should be enough time to make your contacts and avoid overwhelming yourself with work.

### SHORT COURSES THAT DRAW CLIENTS

"Networking Basics for Managers"

"Databases for Competitive Advantage"

"How Safe is your Data?"

"Industrial-Strength Databases for Midsize Manufacturers"

"Getting The Most Out Of Today's Accounting Software"

## Q: What will I get paid for teaching these classes?

**A:** Most extension courses pay a rate based on the number of attendees you attract and the number of hours you teach. Usually any payment will be modest—rarely over a few hundred dollars and often less.

## Q: What about those seminars offered by the big, expensive seminar houses?

**A:** Seminar houses hire instructors to teach courses and usually pay them a daily rate somewhere between $750 and $1,200. To be hired you will need a solid credential similar to those you see in the bios of teachers in the seminar house's current catalogs.

If you sign up to teach for a seminar house, you may be asked to sign a non-compete agreement that prevents you from working directly for any clients you meet through the seminar. If your main reason for teaching is to develop new clients negotiate this clause out of your contract, if possible. If it can't be removed, at least limit its scope so that it lets you perform services other than teaching for clients you meet through the seminars.

## PROMOTE YOURSELF TO "EXPERT" WRITING ARTICLES

The business and trade press are always hungry for material. You can greatly increase your visibility to both local and national clients by publishing articles on your topic of expertise in business publications.

# HOW TO GET AN ARTICLE PUBLISHED IN THE TRADE PRESS

### Locate Publications That Cater To Your Clientele.

- *Don't ignore limited circulation and specialty business publications. You'll find dozens of these listed in ULRICH'S INTERNATIONAL DIRECTORY OF PUBLICATIONS, found in the reference department of most larger libraries.*

- *Write to the feature editor at any magazine you're considering. Ask for a copy of their editorial guidelines and, if the magazine is not available on newsstands, request a sample copy.*

- *Examine an issue of the magazine. Is your target client likely to read it? Does the magazine include material written by consultants? Could you write with an approach and tone similar to what you find in the articles in the sample issue?*

### Choose A Problem-Solving Topic That Will Interest Your Target Client.

- *Make sure your idea has not already been done by doing a keyword search in the electronic business periodicals index you can find at a college or large public library.*

- *Outline your article.*

- *Write a one-page letter to the editor describing your article and asking if he or she is interested in seeing it.*

- *If an editor asks you to write an article based on your proposal, meet your deadline.*

### Make Sure Your Readers Can Find You

- *Include your business name and full contact information with your article and urge the editor to print it at the end of the article.*

- *Give the periodical written permission to pass on your name and phone number to any readers who want to get in touch with you.*

## NEWSLETTERS

You'll often find newsletters described as a hot marketing technique. But few computer consultants have the time or ability to produce the kind of newsletter that is a useful selling tool.

Writing your own newsletter is time consuming and only recommended for those who already have some experience with writing. If you aren't an accomplished writer, you may get as good results from buying a newsletter from a newsletter service and customizing it with your logo and a few lines addressed to your clients as you do from writing one on your own.

Consultant-written newsletters are most effective for consultants who are trying to promote themselves into the role of management expert. Such newsletters may even be profit centers for these consultants, since management-oriented newsletters that promise readers up-to-the-minute material they can't get anywhere else may sell for as much as $400 a year. But producing this kind of newsletter can be a full-time job and newsletter veterans report that even with the hefty subscription price, printing, mailing, and advertising costs usually eat up their profits on a first year subscription. They only start making money when they retain their subscribers year after year.

The fact sheet you'll find on the next page gives you tips on how to get the most out of your newsletter.

## WHAT ARE EFFECTIVE MARKETING MATERIALS?

The following are some types of marketing materials used by computer consultants. But be careful that you don't fall into the common trap of thinking that designing marketing materials like a business card or brochure *is* marketing. Marketing is what you do that makes the recipient want to keep the card or refer to the brochure.

### BUSINESS CARDS

The function of a business card is to let people know how to reach you and to remind them of what you specialize in. Every card should have your address, phone and fax number, and any email address you check on a daily basis. Include one line that summarizes your specialty. Don't hang up on giving yourself fancy job titles. If you are a one-person firm, it's best to omit titles entirely and simply give your name.

# NEWSLETTER TIPS

- ᴆ *Newsletters work slowly.*

- ᴆ *Newsletters are best at keeping you in touch with existing clients and people who have already met you face to face.*

- ᴆ *Mailing newsletters quarterly may be as effective as mailing one every month.*

- ᴆ *A badly written newsletter is worse than no newsletter.*

- ᴆ *Don't mail blindly. Mail only to those who can hire you or refer you good clients.*

- ᴆ *Drop a name from your list if you don't get some feedback that suggests your newsletter is having an effect.*

- ᴆ *Newsletters are most effective for selling highly specialized services that clients have difficulty locating. Newsletters rarely sell generic services.*

- ᴆ *Include articles that readers will want to cut out and save.*

- ᴆ *If you don't write well or don't have the time to write your own articles, consider buying a canned newsletter from a newsletter provider and customizing it with your own cover page. This is effective only if the subject matter of the canned newsletter dovetails with the kind of work you do.*

- ᴆ *When buying canned newsletters, make sure you have protection for your territory and that you understand the supplier's orientation so that you don't end up mailing out articles that recommend strategies or products you don't support.*

- ᴆ *If your newsletter doesn't generate new business that is directly attributable to it within six months, rethink your strategy.*

- ᴆ *The biggest problem with newsletters as a marketing tool is this: they eat up so much time and effort that when you finally put an issue in the mail, you may feel that you've done your marketing for the month and neglect other more powerful techniques*

Unless you are willing to pay for professional logo design, it's best to stick to a stock design that you can pick out of a catalog at any copy shop.

Nobody hires a consultant because they have a ritzy business card. So don't waste energy obsessing about this part of your image.

### LETTERHEAD STATIONARY AND ENVELOPES

Again, choose either a tried and true canned format, or use the services of a trained graphic designer. Laser-designed letterhead is adequate for almost all computer consultants. Preprinted four-color stationery designed to be customized with your own laser printer is available from specialty companies like Paper Direct. But this stationary costs five times what regular stationary does, and may result in an image that is graphically overwhelming—paradoxically undercutting the professional image you want to build. If you do opt for this kind of stationary, chose an understated pattern.

> # GOTCHA!!
> ## The Term "Engineer" Has Special Meaning
>
> In some states it is illegal to call yourself an engineer unless you have passed state-supervised licensing exams.
>
> So avoid calling yourself a "systems engineer" or "computer engineer" unless you are legally entitled to that designation.

### BROCHURES

A greatly overrated marketing tool for consultants, the brochure is expensive to produce, dates easily, and is worth doing only if you have impressive credentials or do very specialized work.

The main function of a brochure is to remind prospects of your credentials, your track record, and the services you provide, *after* they've met with you. If you don't have impressive credentials and a solid track record, there's no point in putting together a brochure. Even if you do, the brochure functions best as a memory-jogger. It is rarely an effective tool for introducing yourself to unknown prospects. If you do choose to use a brochure, make sure you get professional help designing it. Nothing looks worse than a cheaply printed brochure designed by an amateur.

## RÉSUMÉS

Many consultants believe résumés are only appropriate for employees. But clients will want to know where you came from and what you've done to give yourself the right to call yourself an expert. So if you are just starting out, a résumé may be more effective in making sales than a self-puffing, vague brochure or an almost-empty client list.

If you are just starting out and it bothers you to provide clients with a résumé, call it a "project list" and describe the work you did on your last few salaried jobs as "projects."

The important thing, of course, is to make sure that whatever you call it, the document in question strengthens your credential and suggests to clients that you can do the jobs they need done.

Formal résumés are appropriate for contract programmers. (You'll find a sample resume, designed to point up technical skills, in Chapter Five.) Keep any résumé you use under two pages in length and highlight your technical and product experience as much as possible.

---

### DO YOU NEED A BROCHURE. . .

- Do most consultants in your niche use them?
- Are your credentials and experience impressive enough to stand out on a brochure?
- Can you afford to have your brochure designed by a professional?
- Will you be able to use the same brochure for a year or more, or will it need constant revision?

### OR AN ALTERNATIVE?

Useful alternatives to a typeset brochure include:
- A business card that includes a line describing your specialty
- A technology-slanted résumé
- A project list
- A client list
- A Paper Direct laser-generated brochure printed on demand

## CONSULTING CONTROVERSY

### "I" or "We?"

Should you give your company a name that contains the word "Associates?"

Should you write and speak about your business as "We" rather than "I"?

Should you put your company name rather than a personal name on business cards and brochures?

**YES:** You want to relate to clients as a business, not as an individual, and in a few years there may be other people working for (or at least with) you.

**NO:** This strategy will backfire on you if your client discovers that your only "associate" is your cat. If a client is unwilling to work with a one-person firm, pretending to be larger than you are is not going to help—indeed, it will only confirm the client's suspicion that one-person firms are unreliable. Most clients don't distinguish between one-person and ten-person consulting firms, considering both "small" in contrast to the truly "large" consulting firms that employ hundreds or even thousands of so-called consultants.

## PROJECT LISTS

The one-page project list is a more effective and flexible marketing tool for most consultants than the brochure. Printed on your regular stationary with your computer printer, the project list gives client names and briefly describes the projects you have completed for each client.

You can arrange the projects on a client list by

- Technology.

- Industry.

- Application involved.

- Client name.

Use the order in which you sort your client list to draw attention to something you want to highlight, for example, your experience in a hot technology or your Fortune 100 clientele. A chronological presentation is not recommended as it looks too much like a résumé.

Using client names is most effective when your clients are large, well-known companies. Make sure that any client you cite by name will give you a good recommendation if a potential client calls. If there is any question about whether a client will react badly to having their project described on your client list use a generic descriptor rather than the company name.

---

### SAMPLE CLIENT LIST ENTRIES

| PROJECT TYPE | CLIENT |
| --- | --- |
| Smalltalk Software Development | Medical Claim System Fortune 100 Insurer. |
| Auto parts inventory system | AutoSource Inc. Susan Bedford, VP Mfg. |
| C++ Software Development | General Motors, Detroit Customer Information Systems |

# WORKSHEET: Jump-start Your Marketing Efforts

*Use the following worksheet to plan the marketing efforts you'll pursue over the next month.*

1. List the phone numbers and current job titles of the three best bosses you've had in the past and of three coworkers you've had good relationships with who have moved to other companies.

2. If you haven't haven' t contacted these people within the last six months call them up, lunch with them, or send them a friendly note telling them what you're up to.

3. Do you have an up-to-date business card? If not, get some made. Make sure that your consulting specialty is clearly indicated on the card.

4. Make it a goal to hand out ten cards every week. Don't be too selective about whom you give them to. If possible, jot a note on the back of the card reminding the recipient who you are.

5. Read the business section of your newspaper or a trade magazine and find one meeting you can attend this month that will bring you into contact with people who might have a use for your services.

6. At the meeting, set a goal of talking to three professionals and seeing if you can get them to tell you about their work. Extra bonus points if you get them to reveal their biggest current headache.

7. Investigate the existence of an appropriate consulting organization in your region. Look for listings in the business section of the paper, call PC users groups, or contact high profile professional groups like IEEE and ask if they sponsor such a group.

8. Attend a meeting of consultants. At the meeting talk to three other consultants and learn as much as you can from them about how they got started and what kinds of work they do for clients.

9. If you are interested in subcontracting, ask other consultants if there are any brokers or consulting companies they'd recommend or avoid. Write down the names they give you as such firms often have similar names and are easy to confuse.

## CREATE YOUR OWN CUSTOM MARKETING PLAN

1. Review the "Marketing Principles for Consultants" you'll find summarized on Page 119.

2. Use the "Sharpening Your Market Message" Worksheet on Page 117 to define the message that will be the focus of your marketing efforts.

3. Review the Table of "Niches and Effective Marketing Techniques" on Page 129 and choose the techniques you'll focus on.

4. Review the specifics of those techniques.

5. Prepare any necessary marketing materials (see Page 146 for details.)

6. Set up a schedule of marketing activities for the next month.

7. Keep to your schedule.

8. Don't judge your results until you hit the seven-month mark.

9. Remember to keep on marketing even when clients start pouring in.

## COLD CALLING—FIRST AID FOR THE AILING PRACTICE

Up until now all the marketing techniques we've been discussing have been slow-acting ones whose goal was to build an awareness of who you are and what you do in the mind of potential clients. But what if you need some clients fast?

The solution may be cold calling.

Cold calling means telephoning dozens if not hundreds of businesses using a prepared script, in the hopes of finding the one or two that need your services. It is not for the shy or squeamish. It is not fun. But it works.

## WHEN IS COLD CALLING APPROPRIATE?

- Cold calling is appropriate when you can come up with a list of at least fifty businesses that might need your services.

- Cold calling is appropriate when you provide narrowly defined services, not generic ones. For example, you are more likely to succeed selling "remote back-up services" through cold calling than "PC support."

- Cold calling is appropriate when you have an easily recognized, well respected credential.

> **HOT TIP!**
>
> Often a spouse or significant other may do a better job selling your services over the phone than you can do yourself.

- Cold calling is appropriate when you have nothing to lose by alienating a good proportion of those you contact.

# HOW TO COLD CALL

## COME UP WITH A PHONE LIST

☎ Ask a reference librarian to help you locate useful business directories. Create your own phone list from these directories.

☎ Call up list brokers and buy carefully targeted phone lists. You can find a huge selection of list brokers of all types in *Literary Marketplace*, a reference book found in all public libraries.

☎ Contact your local Chamber of Commerce for directories or phone lists of local businesses and professionals sorted by line of business.

☎ Buy phone lists from closed circulation specialty business magazines.

☎ Buy phone lists from local and national professional associations that your clients might belong to.

☎ If a phone number turns out to be a main switchboard, ask the receptionist a question like, "Can you please tell me the name and telephone extension of your Vice President of MIS?"

## WRITE AN EFFECTIVE SCRIPT

☎ Write out a script and practice using it with a friend who takes the part of a client.

☎ Identify the specialty service or keyword you will use as your door opener. This should be the one single service that your prospect is most likely to know they need.

☎ In the first line of your script you should:

1. Identify yourself by name

2. Cite your specialty

3. State that you'd like a few minutes of their time to describe what you do or to offer them your services.

## RESPOND CORRECTLY

☎ If the prospect is not interested in your services, thank them politely for their time and hang up.

☎ If the prospect shows interest, respond to any questions and then offer to set up a face-to-face meeting.

### COLD CALLING PRINCIPLES

- You are looking for people who already know they need the kinds of services you sell.

- You are merely locating prospects, not selling over the phone.

- Your goal is to set up a face to face interview which you can discuss the prospect's needs further.

## PREPARE FOR THE REST OF THE CONVERSATION:

☎ Write out some sentences which emphasize the benefits clients get from your services. You will refer to this list *only if* the client asks for more information.

☎ Write out brief descriptions of the kinds of projects you've done in the past. Refer to this list *only if* the client asks for this information.

☎ Keep your schedule handy and remember that your goal is to set up an appointment *not* to sell on the phone.

## SAMPLE COLD CALLING DIALOGUES

**CONSULTANT:**  *Hello, I'm Joe Schmoe. I'm an expert at automating the widget honing process and I'm calling to offer you my services.*

**PROSPECT:**  *We don't hone widgets here and have no intention of starting.*

**CONSULTANT:**  *Well, I appreciate you taking the time to speak to me. Thanks!  <pause for reply if any, then hang up.>*

**WHY?**  *If the prospect isn't interested, you should politely end the conversation as quickly as possible.*

**PROSPECT:**  *We don't use consultants. But if you want, you can send me some literature.*

**CONSULTANT:**  *That's all right. Thank you for your time. <pause, hang up.>*

**WHY?**  *Clients will often ask you to "send literature" as a polite way of getting rid of you. Don't waste your time or money responding to this stall, but terminate the call politely as you would with any other uninterested prospect.*

**PROSPECT**  *We've got a pretty good in-house widget honing staff here. <pause>  Can you tell me something about your background?*

**CONSULTANT:**    *After getting my Masters degree in Computer Science, I spent ten years at Megacorp. My most significant achievement there was implementing a real-time control system that cut the time spent on Widget Honing by half. <slight pause for feedback> I've been consulting since 1992 and have completed three major projects. In the latest, at Fortune Company, I was able to introduce a new technology that cut annual production costs by 30%. <pause and allow feedback>*

**WHY?**      *Reply to requests for more information with a carefully scripted mixture of your credentials and the benefit clients get from your services.*

☎

**PROSPECT:**    *Widget honing, eh? I was just talking about widget honing with a friend of mine last week. He works over at StressCorp–for now anyway. But with all their layoffs, who knows? Isn't it something the way they're laying folks off there?*

**CONSULTANT:**    *It sure is. Does your company hone its own widgets?*

**WHY?**      *Be careful not to get led off into chit-chat. If the prospect wants to talk about some irrelevancy for a while, let them–you don't want to come across as rude. But do your best to return the conversation to the subject at hand–determining if the prospect needs your services.*

☎

**PROSPECT:**    *We don't hone widgets here, but you might want to talk to Sally Something over at Bigger Co. I recall hearing that they're gearing up to do a big project in that area.*

**CONSULTANT:** *Thank you! I'll certainly call her. Can you tell me how she spells her last name? <writing it down> Thanks! Can I mention that you referred me? Great! Thanks, I really appreciate your help. <pause, hang up>*

**WHY?** *Be alert for any leads prospects might give you and be sure to check them out. Ask permission to mention the referrer's name since you have a much better chance of getting through if you can say, "Tom Prospect suggested I call you."*

**PROSPECT:** *We've been meaning to look into getting some help with our widget system. It's been a headache for years, but it's hard to know what direction to take with it, especially, with this new Windows upgrade on the horizon. Would you recommend the new release of Widgets for Windows?*

**CONSULTANT:** *Widgets for Windows is one solution we sometimes recommend for reengineering aging widget systems, but I can't really give you a complete answer until I know more about how you do business.*

*I'd be happy to come over for a free hour-long consultation where we could discuss this further. Once I have a better idea of how your current system works I may be able to identify the bottlenecks that are causing most of your headaches and show you a couple of cost effective approaches to reengineering them. <pause> When would be convenient for you?*

**WHY?** *Resist the temptation to start analyzing problems or giving solutions over the phone. Use the prospect's descriptions of problems to lead into setting an appointment. If the prospect is not* *willing to set up an appointment, then the requests for help or information were probably just politeness–or an attempt to take advantage of free advice.*

**PROSPECT:**    *What do you charge?*

**CONSULTANT:**  *It's hard to discuss rates before looking into your needs and the special requirements of your business. However, I can assure you our rates are very competitive.*

*Since we specialize in widget honing systems, we're able to reuse a lot of the code and software tools we've developed on earlier projects. This cuts down the time it takes us to get results. If you're interested, I'd be happy to drop by your office sometime for a brief meeting in which we could explore your needs further. <pause for feedback> When are you free?*

**WHY?**    *It's often a good idea to avoid discussions of rates until you have a better idea of what kind of assignment is involved.*

**PROSPECT:**    *What do you charge?*

**CONSULTANT:**  *My standard rate is $65 dollars an hour.*

**WHY?**    *If you bill a standard hourly rate it may be appropriate to mention it up front to save yourself from wasting time on those who cannot afford your services.*

**PROSPECT:** *I don't really have time to discuss this now, but I do have some concerns about our current widget honing system. Can you send me some literature?*

**CONSULTANT:** *I'd be happy to. I'll send you some information about my company and the kind of work we do and call you back next week after you've had a chance to review it. <pause to allow feedback, then make sure to get accurate address information>*

**WHY?** *It is appropriate to send literature if a prospect's behavior gives you the feeling that they are interested in learning more about your services. But since many of these requests are stalls, keep costs down by keeping any literature pack you send out simple.*

# WHAT DO YOU SEND WHEN THE PROSPECT SAYS, "Send me Some Literature?"

### ESSENTIAL ITEMS:

- A brief presentation of your credentials.

- A statement of what kinds of work you specialize in and, if appropriate, the technologies you employ.

- An up-to-date client list or résumé.

### SUGGESTED ITEMS:

- A questionnaire to help the client clarify his needs and a postage-paid envelope for reply.

- A "free offer" for an on-site requirements analysis with a postage-paid envelope for reply.

- Testimonials from satisfied clients that you have gotten permission to copy and include.

- Reprints of articles you've published about your specialty.

- Blurbs from reviews of any books you have written.

- Announcements of upcoming lectures you are giving.

- Mention of your association with any professional groups that establish your professionalism and the length of time you've been a professional. (E.g., "Independent Computer Consultants Association—member since 1988.")

- Mention of your participation in relevant vendor programs. (E.g., Microsoft Solutions Provider, Certified Novell Engineer.)

# 5 BROKERED COMPUTER CONSULTING

**CHAPTER OBJECTIVE**

**Work through large consulting firms and contract brokers**

- Learn what kinds of consultants find work through brokers

- Understand your options as a W-2 Contractor

- Find out what to expect when you deal with a broker

- Discover how to negotiate with consulting firms to get the best contract terms

- Understand clauses commonly found in brokered contracts

N ot every computer consultant is a raging entrepreneur. Many of those who call themselves computer consultants find their clients simply by making a few phone calls to large consulting firms or contract brokers.

# WHAT IS BROKERED CONSULTING?

### Q: *What is a broker?*

**A:**  A broker is a person or company that places consultants on long-term contracts with a variety of clients. In return for this service the broker takes a percentage of every dollar the consultant earns on the job.

### Q: *What is a consulting firm?*

**A:**  Many companies that call themselves "consulting firms" are simply contract brokers. They provide no service beyond placing consultants on projects. Other consulting firms are companies run by computer consultants who subcontract out pieces of their projects to other consultants. A third kind of consulting firm is a large company with offices around the nation that sometimes acts like a broker and places individual contractors on projects, but at other times provides its clients with entire project teams complete with managers , turnkey  software solutions, or outsourcing support.

### Q: *Where do I find a broker or consulting firm?*

**A:**  Many advertise heavily in the Classified Section of the Sunday newspaper. However, the better firms recruit mainly by word of mouth. They get their new consultants from referrals provided by consultants who already work for them.

### Q: *Are broker firms regulated in any way?*

**A:** No. Anyone can call themselves a "consulting firm" and none of the "professional" associations of brokers or consulting firms enforces a code of ethics. As a result, many brokers and consulting firms indulge in questionable business tactics. You will need to talk to experienced consultants in your region to find out which local firms are safe to deal with and which ones should be avoided.

> **Note—**
> *We'll be referring to brokers and consulting firms interchangeably in this chapter.*

### Q: If a broker firm finds me a contract, how do I get paid?

**A:** You will sign a contract with the broker that specifies what rate you will be paid and when you'll receive payment. You will negotiate your rate with the *broker*, not the client, and the *broker*, not the client, will be legally bound to pay you. The broker will negotiate a separate contract with the client which you will never see. Brokers usually take 25-35% of every dollar they bill a client for your services.

### Q: I contacted a consulting firm, but they insisted that they only work with W-2 employee consultants. Is this common?

**A:** Yes. See Chapter Two for a discussion of the reasons why many consultants are forced to work on brokered contracts as employees. There are regional differences in how prevalent this is. In some markets clients are more tolerant of having contractors work as independents than others and local broker firms will set their policies accordingly. Some brokers will insist that you be incorporated before they will place you as an independent contractor. Others may force you to wait for payment until the client pays them, to increase your risk and decrease your appearance of being a covert employee.

### Q: Can I work some brokered contracts as an independent and others as a W-2 consultant?

**A:** Yes. But if you are doing identical work on both types of contracts, if you are audited, the IRS may reclassify your independent work as employee work. If that happens your clients will be assessed stiff penalties.

### Q: Why go through all the headaches of working with a third party firm?

**A:** Because they have jobs—good ones—many involving months of full-time work at rates from $25-75/hr. And because they can often place you on such a contract within days of first hearing from you. Another reason you may have to deal with brokers is that many large corporate clients will only hire consultants through third party firms.

## WHAT CAN GO WRONG?

It's important to check out the local reputation of any consulting firm that might approach you with an offer. If you deal with an unethical consulting firm, any of the following may happen:

💣 You may be told that your résumé has been submitted for a job when it has not. The unethical firm does this to keep your résumé from being submitted by a competing firm. That way, a less qualified—and less highly paid—employee of the unethical firm can win the contract.

💣 On out-of-town contracts, you may be promised reimbursement for airline tickets and living expenses you never receive.

💣 The consulting firm may lie to the client about your experience and skills.

💣 You may show up ready to begin a contract—having turned down other work—only to find that the firm has replaced you with an employee who will work for a much smaller cut of the billing.

💣 You may be promised a contract but not receive the paperwork until you've begun work—at which point you'll discover that the contract specifies a lower rate than what you were promised orally, or includes some other unacceptable terms.

💣 You may find that the actual work involved in the contract bears no relationship to what was described to you in the interview. (Though this may be the client's, not the broker's fault.)

💣 You may be paid with bouncing checks—paycheck after paycheck.

💣 You may not be paid at all.

## WORKSHEET: Can *You* Work Through A Broker?

*Use the following questionnaire to determine if it would be worth pursuing brokered contracts.*

1.  Can you program in a currently popular business programming language or can you configure, install, and maintain networks?
    ☐ Yes    ☐ No

2.  Do you have three or more years of recent, paid experience doing this kind of work?
    ☐ Yes    ☐ No

3.  Do you have paid experience using computers in an in-demand application area, such as insurance, banking, manufacturing, or shrink-wrapped software development?
    ☐ Yes    ☐ No

4.  Are you willing to work at the client's premises?
    ☐ Yes    ☐ No

5.  Are you willing to work 40 hour weeks for a single client?
    ☐ Yes    ☐ No

6.  Are you willing to accept W-2 status in return for the guarantee of several months of full-time work at contract rates?
    ☐ Yes    ☐ No

7.  Are you willing to sign a noncompetition clause obligating you to work for the broker if you return to the broker's client?
    ☐ Yes    ☐ No

8.  Are you willing to sign over to the client the rights to any software you develop while working on the contract?
    ☐ Yes    ☐ No

9.  If you intend to work in the U.S. can you prove that you are a U.S. Citizen?
    ☐ Yes    ☐ No

## COMMENTS ON THE "Can You Work Through A Broker" WORKSHEET

Most of the consultants brokers place are contract programmers or people with specialized technical skills such as the ability to install and maintain networks.

In addition, brokers are usually looking for people who have significant amounts of recent paid experience using the programming languages, operating systems, and hardware popular with the large corporate clients who are their primary customers.

Brokers will rarely place managers unless they have heavy-duty technical skills or have had a great deal of experience doing strategic planning or configuration design in a large-scale corporate environment. In general, contract assignments for people with managerial skills are much rarer than those for programmers though they may pay very good rates.

Brokered contracts are often "temporary jobs" that require that you work full-time, on-site, for an open-ended time period. You may have to accept W-2 employee status to get the contract and give up supporting other clients during working hours.

Brokered contracts usually require that you sign a noncompetition clause binding you to work for the broker in the future should you want to return to any client the broker has found for you. They also usually include clauses requiring that you assign the rights to all code developed under the contract to the client for whom it is being developed.

Brokers, like other employers, will ask you to show proof of citizenship before hiring you.

## HOW TO AVOID DISREPUTABLE CONSULTING FIRMS

Because there are abusive consulting firms in the marketplace, take the time to check out any firm you might consider working with. Ask other consultants what firms they'd recommend. Ask managers who hire consultants what firms they like to work with. And be alert to warning signs that suggest problems ahead:

💣 Avoid any firm whose salesperson suggests you do something unethical, for example, telling a client you have experience you really don't have.

💣 Avoid firms whose salespeople pump you for information about firms you used to work for.

💣 Avoid dealing with out-of-town firms that don't maintain local offices and can't give local references.

💣 Don't deal with firms whose salespeople can't understand your résumé.

💣 Refuse to go on an interview for any firm that submits your résumé without first getting your permission.

💣 Don't deal with firms that send you to inappropriate interviews.

💣 Don't work for firms that are not willing to modify abusive contract clauses.

## HOW TO GET THE MOST OUT OF BEING A W-2 CONSULTANT

Many brokers and consulting firms will try to talk you into working as a regular salaried employee, arguing that this status gives you job security and desirable benefits. But salaried work is rarely a good deal for any contractor whose skills are in demand.

If you must work on a W-2 basis, avoid accepting a salaried position. Instead, negotiate with the consulting company to work as an *hourly employee*. Hourly employees give up the promise of job security and benefits in return for a much higher hourly rate similar to what independents get.

This makes sense because true job security is rarely found in any consulting firm and because consultants who work for high hourly rates can buy their own benefits and still come out earning much more than consultants who work for a salary and benefits.

Table 7. Hourly Rate Consulting vs. Regular Salaried Employee Consulting

| Hourly Rate W-2 Consultants | Salaried Consulting Company Employees |
| --- | --- |
| Receive a much higher hourly rate, as much as twice what salaried consultants get | Get paid a salary similar to that paid to regular corporate employees |
| Get paid for every hour worked including overtime | Expected to work a lot of unpaid overtime for clients |
| Get no benefits from the consulting firm but must buy their own | Receive benefits of varying quality including health insurance, life insurance and disability insurance |
| Do not get paid on holidays, sick days or vacations | Get paid holidays, sick days, and vacations |
| End their employment with the consulting firm when the contract with the client terminates and may work for several firms over the course of a year | Must take any consulting assignment the consulting company finds for them or be fired—even if the assignment is several hours away from their home or in another state |
| Usually have more "in-demand" skills and more experience than salaried consulting company employees | Often are sent to fill jobs that do not use their expertise and lead to their skills becoming rusty and obsolete |
| Must pay for their own training classes but are more likely to to attend them | Are usually promised training when recruited—but few report receiving this training |
| Do not have to take another contract unless they want it and may take time off whenever they choose | Will be terminated within a few weeks if the consulting company cannot find them another assignment |
| May claim unemployment if no other contract is offered | Can file for unemployment if laid off for lack of work |

# GOTCHA!!

## *HOURLY RATE CONSULTING IS A MISTAKE...*

- When there is weak demand for your specialty in your region

- When you have mediocre technical skills

In either case, consulting firms can fill any contracts you might qualify for with their own salaried employees and thus won't place you.

## WHAT TO EXPECT WHEN DEALING WITH BROKERS

Here is the usual sequence of events you'll experience when finding work through brokers or consulting firms:

**Initial Contact:** You respond to an ad or are called after being referred by another consultant.

**Request for Résumé:** The broker will discuss your work history and if there seems to be a match with their requirements, they'll ask you to mail or fax in your résumé. When you do, use a résumé slanted to highlight your experience with current technology, not one that stresses business achievements or management experience. Refer to the sample résumé on Page 177 for an example of a résumé formatted in this manner.

You should never give more than one consulting firm permission to submit your résumé to clients. When a client receives two copies of your résumé—with two different rates attached—the chances of your getting the job drop to zero. To avoid having this happen, word the cover letter that accompanies your résumé in a way that makes it clear that you will not interview for an assignment if your résumé is submitted without your explicit approval.

**Initial Interview:** Reputable firms will have their own staff interview you before they send you out on a client interview. You should be wary of firms that do not perform this kind of screening. Reputable firms will also probe for signs of technical competence and verify that you have the experience you claim to have.

***Initial Rate Discussion:*** If the consulting firm expresses interest in working with you, this is the time to make sure they are willing to pay you the rate you want. If the firm says your rate is too high, it is rarely negotiable. However, many firms will suggest in this preliminary phase that they may be able to pay a higher rate than they will actually offer when a real contract comes through.

***Waiting Period:*** Your résumé will go into the broker's database until a contract comes up that no one else on their waiting list can fill. As you would expect, the broker will try to place salaried employees and qualified consultants who have already worked for them in the past before they consider you. If you don't hear anything, check back every two weeks to let the firm's recruiters know that you are still looking for a contract. Do not call more frequently, as you will only label yourself as a pest.

***Contract Call:*** When a contract comes into the firm that they can't fill with one of their regulars, they will begin calling contractors who have the required experience until they locate one who can interview for the position. When you get a call, make sure to ask exactly what technology the job requires, what rate the job will pay, and when it begins, before agreeing to go on an interview, in order to save yourself wasted time and effort.

***Client Interview:*** The consulting firm will set up an interview for you with the client. A consulting firm salesperson may go along with you to the interview to introduce you to the client. This salesperson may or may not sit in during the actual interview itself. The client may ask you when you can start, but should not discuss rates with you. Don't be surprised if the client wants you to start in a day or two.

***Contract Offer from the Consulting Firm:*** If the client wants to hire you, the consulting firm will call you with an offer. At this time you will get a firm rate from the broker and you may be able to negotiate that rate up by a dollar or two an hour.

***Contract Submitted by the Consulting Firm:*** When you accept the contract firm's verbal offer they will send or fax you a contract. You must examine it with great care and negotiate any unacceptable clauses. Reputable firms will negotiate most of these clauses. (You'll find a discussion of these contract clauses on Page 178.) If you cannot negotiate an unacceptable clause into one you can live with, you can reject the contract at this point. Otherwise you should sign it and return a copy to the broker.

**Begin Work for Client:** On the first day of the contract a consulting company representative will probably meet you at the job site. You will then work according to the terms of the contract. The consulting firm may send someone around to drop in on you once every few weeks, although this is usually a purely ritual visit.

**Extend the Contract:** A few weeks before the contract is scheduled to end, you may be asked to extend it and to work for a longer period at the same rate you are currently working for. Acceptance of such extensions may be a condition of the original contract. If you extend the contract in this manner, you will usually just sign a one-page contract extension form and keep on working.

**Terminate the Contract:** If the client does not extend the contract, you will cease working on the date specified in your contract. This will end your connection with both the client and the consulting firm unless the consulting firm offers you another contract.

If you have been working as a W-2 employee and the broker firm cannot offer you another contract, you may ask for a pink slip so that you can file for unemployment. If you have been working as a 1099 contractor, you may not file for unemployment.

## GOTCHA!!

Almost all consulting firm contracts are written in such a way that the client can terminate you without notice for any reason at all.

Common reasons for unilaterally ending a contract include cancellation of the project, the hiring of full time staffers to take over the work you are doing, and not liking the way you do your work.

If you are terminated in this way, there is no appeal and you should not expect the consulting company to do anything on your behalf. If faced with a choice, consulting firms will always do whatever it takes to keep their clients, rather than their contractors, happy.

## Example 4. Why You Do Better with an Hourly Rate

| Hourly Consultant | Salaried Consultant |
|---|---|
| **Scenario #1** | |
| Number of months of work:  9 | Number of months of work: 9 |
| *Three contracts, each three-months long with three different consulting firms.* | *Three assignments. Fired three weeks after the third contract was complete for lack of work.* |
| Potential billable hours:  1,480 | Actual number of weeks employed:  40 |
| *Subtract 64 billable hours lost due to sick days and Holidays* | |
| Actual billable hours:  1,416 | |
| Earnings (@$40/hr):  $56,640 | Annual Salary:        $50,000 |
| | 40 weeks' earnings:  $38,461 |
| Deduct cost of self-paid health, life and disability insurance: $5,700 | Deduct cost of self-paid health insurance for period of unemployment: $1,315 |
| Net earnings for the year: $50,940. | Net earnings for the year: $37,146 |

| Hourly Consultant | Salaried Consultant |
|---|---|
| **Scenario # 2** | |
| Period worked:  All year | Period worked: All year |
| Hours worked:  1,920 | Hours worked:  2,190 |
| *40/wk, minus holidays, vacation and sick days* | *Includes five hours a week average overtime* |
| Income @$40/hr        $76,800 | Salary          $50,000 |
| Minus cost of benefits:    5,700 | Benefits:            9,000 |
| Actual income:              71,100 | Actual income:   59,000 |
| Effective rate/hr: $37 | Effective rate/hr:  $27 |

***Wait Out Noncompete Agreements:*** All consulting firm contracts oblige you to work through the firm if you want to return to the clients they have found for you within some period of time after you end your relationship with the consulting firm. This time period usually begins when you end your contract. You should expect to honor these agreements. (See further discussion of noncompetition clauses on Page 179.) Other consulting firms will ask you to inform them about any pre-existing noncompete agreements before they offer to place you.

## CONTRACT CONSULTING QUESTIONS AND ANSWERS

**Q: When I'm looking for a contract can I deal with more than one broker at a time?**

**A:** Yes, in fact, it's recommended that you sign up with several, since each firm will only submit one candidate for each contract it hears about. But if you are registered with more than one consulting firm, it's essential that you insist that they not submit your résumé to a client before contacting you and asking your permission. This is to avoid having your résumé submitted to the same client by two competing firms.

**Q: At the company where I have my contract, the employees take an hour lunch period and get paid for a 35 hour week. Can I take a shorter lunch period and bill for a full forty hours?**

**A:** In almost all cases the answer is "yes," and many consultants do this. However you should discuss this with the consulting firm before you sign the contract.

**Q: Everyone where I'm working is a contractor, including the project leader. Some of these people have been working as contract consultants in this same department for three years. Is this unusual?**

**A:** This is very common now that so many companies have become obsessive about cost cutting. The challenge for you as a consultant is to avoid getting sucked into an employee state of mind. Though it's easy to feel like an employee, you aren't one. You'll get no promotions and will be let go the day the company doesn't need you anymore. Make sure you are getting paid enough to buy yourself benefits and save for retirement, and keep your skills current so that you'll be able to find a new job when this long-term contract ends.

**Q: My client wants me to stay on for six more months. I'd like to extend but what do I do about my plans for vacation this summer?**

**A:** When you extend, tell your client that you will need to take a week or two off as you've already made plans. Most clients can handle this.

**Q: I signed a contract with a broker, but after I started work they told me that the client had changed the terms under which I would have to work and that they were going to have to cut my rate. Can they do this?**

**A:** Legally, they cannot do this if you have a written contract. However, large corporate clients know that consulting firms are not going to bite the hands that feed them, and occasionally do breach their the contracts with the consulting firms and impose new terms on them.

Sometimes client companies announce that they will no longer pay consultants overtime but will expect them to put in a so-called "Professional Day" which includes any necessary overtime—unpaid. This condition may be imposed on all contract consultants working for the client. This kind of abuse is occurring more and more as companies move towards replacing whole departments with contractors. If it happens to you, attempt to resolve it through candid discussions with your client and the broker before you turn to a lawsuit, since a lawsuit, no matter how justified is likely to end your relationship with the client and broker for good.

## Example 5.  A Sample Résumé for Brokered Consulting

```
Matthew Frumpkin
123 Beazle Drive
Potemkin, CA  90789
806 123-4567

RECENT CONSULTING PROJECTS

Smalltalk          Client: Abysmal Engineering. Developed real-time
                   control system for Widget Honing manufacturing
                   process using Digitalk Smalltalk for OS/2.
                   July-September, 1995.

Powerbuilder       Client: Widgitech.  Floor control data collection
                   system running on Novell LAN. July-September,
                   1995.

C++                Client: Real-time Environmentals, Inc. Automated
                   Widget honing processor using Borland C++. Data
                   uploaded to a Sybase database. January '95-June
                   '95.

OOP Training       Client: IRN. Taught two week seminar on "Mastering
                   OOP Buzzwords" to project level managers at seven
                   company sites. July-November 1994.

EMPLOYMENT HISTORY

Tecnoid, Inc.      Team leader, OOP development, responsible for
                   completing Smalltalk and C++ widget honing pilot
                   projects on DOS and OS/2 platforms. 1991-1994

Huge Aircraft      Consultant Engineer in charge of process control
                   planning,  1988-1991

SOFTWARE EXPERIENCE

        Digitalk Smalltalk          ASM

        C++                         C (Microsoft and Borland)

        OS/2                        Novell LAN Networking

        UNIX                        MOTIF


EDUCATION

BSCS               California Institute of Technology, 1987.
MBA                University of California at Berkeley, 1991.
HighTech Seminars  Intro to Smalltalk, Advanced Smalltalk,
                   Designing Smalltalk Applications.
```

# BROKER CONTRACT CLAUSES AND WHAT THEY MEAN

Broker contracts come in all shapes and sizes and feature all sorts of legal verbiage. What they have in common is that they are drafted by the broker's lawyer to serve the broker's interest, and almost always include some wording that you must remove or alter.

We'll be discussing many of the clauses commonly found in consulting contracts later in Chapter Six. Here we're going to look at clauses that have special meaning when you find them in a broker's contract. We'll ignore specific wording because the wording in broker contract clauses can vary so greatly, and concentrate instead on what it is that the clause is intended to do.

## DEFINITION OF STATUS

**What It Does:** Define you as an independent contractor, subcontractor, hourly rate employee waiving benefits, or salaried employee with benefits.

## What To Watch Out For:

💣 Does the status on the contract match what you agreed to orally?

💣 Don't accept W-2 work if you perform similar work as a 1099 contractor unless you have thought through the consequences.

## SCOPE OF WORK

**What It Does:** Indicates start and end dates for your contract.

## What To Watch Out For:

💣 Some contracts include wording in the scope of work clause that obligates you to accept any extensions of the contract at the rate that

> ## GOTCHA!!
> ### NEVER WORK WITHOUT A SIGNED CONTRACT
>
> Many of the worst broker abuses can be avoided if you insist on signing a written contract before beginning work. If you wait until the first day of the job to sign the contract, you may find that it doesn't match the verbal agreements you have hewed out. You then risk alienating the client and blackening your own reputation if you back out.
>
>

appears in the original contract. This can be a problem because consulting firm contracts are infamous for being extended for months, years, and even decades! Make sure that there is a mechanism in the contract that allows for renegotiation of rates within a reasonable time period—say a year.

## SCHEDULE OF PAYMENT

**What It Does:** Specifies when you will be paid.

**What To Watch Out For:**

💣 If you are working as a W-2 consultant and the broker is getting the customary 25-35% of your billing dollar, insist that you be paid on a regular biweekly schedule that does not depend on the broker first receiving payment from the client. Corporate clients pay notoriously slowly. If brokers insist that you wait for payment until they are paid, insist that they take a much smaller cut of the billing in return for their much smaller risk.

## OWNERSHIP OF THE FRUITS OF THE CONTRACT

**What It Does:** Assigns all copyrights to work you do on the job to the client. This is a standard clause. While work created by employees legally becomes the property of the employer, work created by independent contractors remains the property of the contractor unless specifically signed over in a written contract. You will find that most contracts for both employee and independent brokered consulting include wording giving the client the rights to code you create for them. Most clients demand this and there is no point in negotiating it unless you will be using your own libraries of pre-existing code as part of the development effort.

**What To Watch Out For:**

💣 If you will be using your own pre-existing code libraries, make sure that you include wording in the contract that makes it clear you are not transferring the copyright to those libraries to the client.

## NONCOMPETITION CLAUSE

**What It Does:** Forces you to work through the same consulting firm on any subsequent contracts you may get with the client until the expiration of some stated period of time. This is a standard clause and you may have to agree to some version of it. But many consulting firms write abusive versions of this clause which must be renegotiated.

### What to watch out for:

💣 Noncompetes that last for much too long. Legitimate time periods for noncompetition clauses are six months to a year. Anything longer is abusive.

💣 Noncompetes that only begin after you end your connection with the consulting firm and include *all* clients you have served while working for the consulting firm. A fair noncompete extends to the single client you have done work for and the noncompetition period begins as soon as you stop working for that client—even if you are working elsewhere through the same broker.

💣 Noncompetes that extend to all divisions of a Fortune 500 firm when you have worked only in a single division. Fair noncompetes should extend, at most, to a single division, since many large companies have dozens of divisions in many different locations which function like separate businesses. Most broker firms only have connections in a limited subset of these divisions and your noncompete should only extend to the divisions where they have good connections.

💣 Noncompetes that extend to all companies at which you have been marketed, not just companies in which you have accepted contracts. This is an abusive clause which could be interpreted as forcing you to work for a consulting firm simply because it mass mailed your résumé to every shop in town!

> **TIP—**
>
> If you have strong personal contacts at a firm where a broker has found you a contract, and if those contacts are not involved in the broker's contract, explicitly exclude your contacts, by name, department and division, from the scope of the noncompete clause, so that you can work directly for them should they call you later with work.

### TERMINATION

***What It Does:*** Specifies the conditions under which the client may terminate you. Specifies the conditions under which you may end the contract. It may specify penalties if you end the contact early. Most brokered contracts contain wording that allows the client to bail out at any time without a penalty. This clause may not be negotiable because clients may insist on it as a condition of working with the consulting firm.

If you are a W-2 consultant, it is appropriate to specify that you can leave the contract if you give two weeks notice.

### What To Watch Out For:

💣 Contracts that don't allow *you* some way out of a long-term contract without penalty in case some unforeseen situation emerges that makes this necessary.

💣 Contracts that oblige you to pay cash penalties if you leave a contract early.

## THE BROKER'S VIEW

Up until now, we've been looking at brokered consulting strictly from the consultant's viewpoint and focusing on the abuses consultants have to watch out for. But not all brokers are sleazy. Building a relationship with an ethical broker may make the difference between failing and succeeding at your consulting career. So before we leave this topic, it's worth spending a moment considering the broker's side of the relationship.

### WHAT GOOD BROKERS DO FOR CONSULTANTS

- Good brokers market fifty-two weeks a year, year in and year out. They keep abreast of what's happening in dozens of local businesses.

- Good brokers pay consultants every two weeks though they often must wait months to collect from the client.

- Good brokers pay the overhead expenses associated with staffing their offices, renting those offices, and recruiting new consultants, though when their consultants aren't working, they don't earn a dime.

- In short, good brokers work hard and earn their cut of the consultant's hourly rate.

# THE CONSULTANT FROM HELL
## ☠ BROKER VERSION ☠

- ☠ The consultant from hell calls daily. He's 18 years old, has never held a paid programming job, and threatens to sue if the broker doesn't find him a job.

- ☠ When the broker schedules a client interview with the consultant's permission, the consultant from hell does not show up for the interview.

- ☠ The consultant from hell accepts a contract but quits three weeks into the job explaining that she's found a full-time position.

- ☠ The consultant from hell displays a dazzling knowledge of buzzwords but six weeks into the contract it becomes clear he cannot do the job.

- ☠ The consultant from hell spends twenty minutes a day on the phone with her boyfriend, takes 40 minute coffee breaks, and calls in sick every Friday.

- ☠ The consultant from hell does not track his hours and does not submit required time sheets, and then complains about payment problems.

- ☠ The consultant from hell gets all his work from brokers, puts no effort into any marketing efforts of his own, does just enough work to get by, upgrades his skills only when the broker offers free training classes, and whines constantly about how unfair it is that "his" money is going into the broker's pocket.

- ☠ Every broker deals with "consultants from hell" on a daily basis. So when you introduce yourself to a reputable broker, a big part of your job is going to be convincing them that you're not one of THEM.

# WORKSHEET: Check Your Brokered Contract

*Use the following checklist to make sure that you haven't overlooked something important in a contract given to you by a broker or consulting firm:*

1. What employment status is specified in this contract?

2. What rate will you be paid?

3. How will you be paid for overtime?

4. When will you receive payment?

5. Is there an end date specified for the contract?

6. Is there wording in the contract obligating you to extend indefinitely?

7. Under what conditions can you terminate the contract?

8. What happens if you have to get out of the contract because of a family health emergency, spouse's relocation, or other unexpected situation?

9. Are you going to be using your own code libraries? Have you specifically excluded them from the ownership clause?

10. To which potential clients does the noncompetition clause apply?

11. When does the noncompetition period begin?

12. Have you limited the time period of the noncompetition clause to a year or less?

13. Are there pre-existing business contacts you'd like to exclude from this noncompetition clause?

# 6 HOW TO WIN CONTRACTS

**CHAPTER OBJECTIVE**

**Turn prospects into clients**

- Make the most of your first meeting with any potential client
- Overcome the bad habits that keep consultants from listening and speaking effectively
- Conduct your initial interview in a way that gives you the most information about the client's needs
- Decide if a client is someone with whom you want to do business
- Follow up in a manner that moves your relationship forward
- Close the sale

**Y**our very first contact with any potential client sets the tone for any future interactions. So when you are face-to-face for the first time with someone who might need your skills, it is essential that you make a good impression. But how do you do this? According to many successful consultants, by being a good listener.

That's because when potential clients make the decision of whether or not they want to deal with you again, that decision is almost always based on how comfortable they felt talking to you during that first contact—not on what was discussed.

Unfortunately, many computer professionals make a poor first impression. They have poor listening skills. They are better at giving information than receiving it from others, and they may get carried away by their enthusiasm when sharing what they know. This causes others to perceive them as obnoxious or socially inept.

So before you can sell yourself to a client, you need to take a long, hard look at how good *your* listening skills might be. If they need improvement, make it a high priority to do what you can to teach yourself to be a better listener.

## HOW TO IMPROVE YOUR LISTENING SKILLS

- Use the worksheet on Page 190 to help gauge how good your current listening skills are and to pinpoint the areas where they need improvement.

- Try setting yourself one specific listening goal before entering a casual conversation. For example, when you meet with someone, set yourself the goal of learning three things you don't already know about this person's background.

- If you have a tendency to talk too much, experiment with forbidding yourself to give any information to another person in a casual conversation except in response to a direct question. Make that other person pry the information out of you instead of offering it to them unsolicited.

- To help yourself remember to listen, try using simple reminder techniques. For example, put a ring on a finger on which you don't usually wear one. Then every time you notice the ring, remind yourself to shut up and listen.

- The fastest and most effective way to improve your listening skills is to tape your conversations with others and listen to the playback. It's brutal, but it works.

## INCOMPATIBLE TECHIE COMMUNICATION PROTOCOLS

One important reason that technically skilled people have trouble making a good first impression is that they often use a communications style among themselves that is *not* the style used by the rest of the world.

The data that flows between two people who are using a standard conversational communications protocol is tagged with embedded markers which provide the feedback that maintains an orderly flow of data. These tags may be expressed through body language or may involve repeating information that has just been communicated or providing some other low-content response that signals that the information has been heard. This is time consuming and permits little actual information to be transmitted.

As a result, information-hungry technical people have evolved a set of alternative communication protocols that improve the data transfer rate by cutting out much of the feedback. These protocols make it easier to get information across to other technical people, but they are guaranteed to annoy prospective clients—to say nothing of spouses, children, and friends. So when you head out to begin your networking efforts, make sure you don't fall into using the common—and highly dysfunctional—Techie Communication Protocols you'll see summarized on the next two pages.

## PROTOCOL

## TUI   TALK UNTIL INTERRUPTED

The technical person pours out ideas, assuming that the listener will interrupt if they have something they'd like to say.

This protocol works fine if the person with whom you are speaking is also programmed to use it. But it is commonly found only in brilliant programmers—and people who grew up in New York City. Everyone else interprets this kind of high speed burst mode data transmission as a communications failure.

## RESPONSE

## FWO   FLEE WHEN OVERWHELMED

The listener in a TUI situation smiles while getting madder and madder at not being given any chance to respond. At the first opportunity, the listener leaves and will take great pains to avoid the speaker from then on.

## PROTOCOL

## RMAC   READ MIND AND CONTINUE

The speaker stops long enough to allow the listener to begin a sentence. However, three words into the listener's reply, the speaker has figured out exactly what the listener was about to say, and to save the listener from wasting time delivering a "null" message begins to deliver the next chunk of data.

## RESPONSE

## FAJ   FLAG AS JERK

The receiver in a RMAC situation takes delivery of each new data chunk as an indication that the speaker has rejected their ideas, concerns, or even, sometimes, right to exist and writes him or her off as an egomaniac.

**PROTOCOL**

# MIB

## MINE IS BIGGER

When someone describes anything, be it a piece of hardware, software, or some problem that has arisen, the speaker responds with the information that his hardware or software are faster and more powerful, or his problems more interesting than those of the speaker.

This terminates conversation as no response is possible.

**PROTOCOL**

# LLA

## LOOP ON LOGIC TIL AGREEMENT

The speaker states a logical argument.

If the listener does not respond with a YACR (You Are Completely Right) the speaker assumes that the listener did not receive all pieces of his logic flow in their correct order and repeats the entire argument from the beginning.

This process continues until the listener delivers the expected YACR or runs screaming out of the room.

**RESPONSE**

# TPA

## TERMINATE WITH PERSONAL ATTACK

The only effective way of terminating the logic loop described above:

The listener delivers a nonlogical outburst that contains an embedded data string such as "You are the most impossible person I've ever known!" or "It's impossible to talk to you. You haven't heard a single word I've said!"

Note—clients and potential clients will NOT terminate an LLA with this signal, but will fall back to the FWO described above.

## WORKSHEET: Rate Your Listening Skills

*Use this worksheet the next time you return from a networking function to see how well you listened to those you met.*

1.      For each person with whom you had a conversation lasting more than a few moments, can you remember:

    a.      Their main point:

    b.      Your main point:

    c.      Something you learned that you didn't know before this conversation:

    d.      Their biggest concern about their business:

2.      Did your main point connect with theirs?

3. What was the most interesting thing they told you?

4. Did you notice the most interesting thing they told you at the time they mentioned it, or only in retrospect?

5. How did you respond to their most interesting point?

6. Did you ask questions that elicited more information about their most interesting point?

7. What was your most significant response to their main point?

8. What was their most significant response to your main point?

9. What did you forget to mention?

## UNDERSTANDING THE "Rate Your Listening Skills" WORKSHEET

***Were You Talking To Each Other?*** If you found that you and the person with whom you were speaking were holding two parallel conversations—ones in which each of you was talking about a topic of interest to themselves which didn't intersect with the other person's topic, you've identified a major area in which to work for improvement.

***Did You Draw People Out?*** Did you respond to the interesting points a speaker made in a way that caused that speaker to expand on those points, or did you use them to lead into saying something that *you* wanted to say, effectively cutting them off? Good listeners never cut other people off, no matter how interesting what they might have to say might be.

***Was the Conversation Balanced?*** Is your memory of the discussion dominated by what you told the other person? Or is it mostly about what they told you? A good listener should maintain a balance between the two, with perhaps a little more emphasis on what the other person told them.

***Did You Catch the Important Stuff?*** Did your ears perk up when the conversation neared a subject close to the speaker's heart, or did you only realize the importance of some topic in retrospect? You're much more likely to succeed with clients if you can cultivate the ability to encourage others to confide in you and respond properly when they introduce subjects of great concern.

***Did You Say What You Wish You Had Said?*** If you came up with a number of things that you now wish you'd said during the conversation but didn't, you may do a good job of listening, but be weak at processing what you hear in "real time." This may not be something you can change. But if your mind works this way, mention these "latecomer" ideas when you next contact the person. This shows that you were listening and that you take the other person's concerns seriously.

Don't despair if your responses to the worksheet show that you are not a good listener. Very few technical people are. However, if your answers here indicate that your output channel is much more highly developed than your input one, make it a priority to improve your listening skills.

## HOW TO FOLLOW UP AFTER FIRST CONTACT

Once you've made a favorable first impression, the key to turning contacts into prospects, is follow-up.

Follow-up refers to anything you do to renew and strengthen your contact with someone you've just met.

Don't rely on fate to bring you back into contact with people who might be able to use your services. Enhance your chances of meeting them again by doing the following:

- Return to any group that seems to have potential and don't make any final decisions about its value until you've attended several meetings.

- When you meet people who seem to share your interests don't be shy. Take the first step towards building a relationship by offering to meet them for lunch.

- Put hot prospects on your quarterly letter/newsletter mailing list.

- Put warm prospects on your "interesting item" phone call list, and call them up once every three months to ask them how they are doing, find out what's new in their business life, and update them on your latest doings.

- Use a computerized contact management system to store names, addresses, and useful information you collect about new people, so you can locate them when you need them.

## SEND FOLLOW-UP MAIL

When you meet a particularly interesting new acquaintance, send them a note to tell them how much you enjoyed meeting them. Briefly refer to what you discussed when you met to remind them of who you are and what you do. The example you'll find on Page 195 gives you an idea of how such a note might be worded.

## TIPS ON WRITING EFFECTIVE FOLLOW-UP LETTERS

If your Mom raised you to send out a written "Thank You" note when you received a Birthday present, you can skip ahead. Otherwise, here are the main points you need to keep in mind:

- 🖅 Use your regular business stationary or a card designed especially for the purpose. You can find "Thank You" notes and other cards designed especially for business use in larger office supply stores.

- 🖅 Writing your note by hand adds a nice personal touch, but don't do it unless your handwriting is legible and you can spell properly without a spellchecker.

- 🖅 Keep your note under a page in length.

- 🖅 Mention something about the other person that shows that you remember who *they* are.

- 🖅 Mention something that reminds them who *you* are.

- 🖅 Don't ever let it sound as if you are hungry for work. Remember, you market best when you look busy.

## YOUR FIRST MEETING WITH A PROSPECT

One glorious day your marketing efforts will result in someone calling you up and asking you for some help. You should respond by setting up a face to face meeting where you can discuss their needs and determine if you can fill them.

A lot will be going on in this first meeting and managing it may be the biggest challenge you face in the whole consulting sales cycle. In it, you must accomplish two different tasks simultaneously: You must find out *what the prospect needs done*, at the same time that you extract the information *you need* to determine whether this is someone you want to do business with. And you must do all this while doing your best to make a favorable impression!

Leaving aside for the time being the issue of how you are going to convince the prospect to buy your services, let's look at what you, the consultant, need to accomplish during the initial interview in order to ensure that if you do get the assignment it will be one worth doing.

## Example 6.  "Nice to Meet You" Letter

```
                        Elmer Sonnenschien
                        MaxiMedia Solutions
                        894 Huckleberry Circle
                        Altoona, PA  03032




September, 21, 1995


Dear Bill,

   Just a brief note to tell you how much I enjoyed our
conversation at Software Development '95.  I thought I was the
only C++ developer in the world who played the nose flute, but
that was before meeting you.  No wonder you've been able to
develop such great multimedia stuff.  If you're ever in Altoona,
give me a holler--and don't forget to bring your nose flute along.

Yours,

Elmer

P.S.   We're doing an exciting project this month writing a set of
       drivers for a new, as yet unannounced, graphics device.
       The best part of the project is that we've been able to add
       some really slick routines to our 64-bit graphics library
       and we're hoping this will give us a jump on developing
       software for what we think is going to be a really exciting
       new technology.
```

# WORKSHEET: What You Have To Find Out At The First Meeting

*Use the following worksheet to fix in your mind the questions you should get answered during your first meeting with a prospect. You may want to make a copy of it and refer to it discreetly during the interview, to make sure you don't forget anything important:*

## STEP ONE: DETERMINE WHAT NEEDS TO BE DONE

1. What problem does the prospect believe needs to be solved?

2. Is this the REAL problem?

3. Does the person you are speaking with have hands-on knowledge of the details of the problem? If not, who does and what is their relationship to this person?

4. Does the prospect already have a formal project design or specification? If there isn't one, is the prospect willing to pay you to produce a detailed specification?

5. Within what time frame does the prospect plan to attack the problem. Can it wait?

## STEP TWO:  DETERMINE IF YOU HAVE A REAL CLIENT

1. Does the person you are speaking with have the authority to buy your services?

2. Is the prospect aware of how much you charge and are they able to pay for your services?

3. Is the prospect comfortable with what you charge?

4. Have you made it clear how much free time you are prepared to give the prospect and when the billing clock will start?

## STEP THREE:  DETERMINE WHAT COMES NEXT

1. Does the prospect want a formal proposal?

2. When should you get back to prospect for the next step?

3. Are there any questions/issues that need be researched on either side before things can proceed?  If so when is the best time to call back and discuss the results?

# COMMENTS ON The "What You Have To Find Out" WORKSHEET

***What's the Problem?*** Never assume that the problem the prospect first describes is the real problem that needs to be solved. Do some probing to see what's really going on before you jump in and explain your approach to a solution. Use the worksheet on Page 199 to help yourself get at what the prospect really needs.

If the person you are speaking with does not have the technical ability to describe the problem, listen carefully to what they tell you, but ask if you can speak to a person with a technical background before you make any formal proposals.

***Qualify the Prospect:*** If the person you are speaking with doesn't have the ability to buy your services, ask them outright if they can introduce you to the person who does.

The best way to determine what resources the prospect has is to ask, "What is your budget for solving this problem?" If there is no budget, or if the budget is much too small to cover what you normally charge, don't waste your time trying to sell yourself to the prospect.

Be alert to signs that suggest that the prospect is seriously motivated to solve the problem not just passing the time shmoozing about it. Stay on track discussing the business issue at hand and avoid chit-chat. You aren't there to make a friend, but to land an assignment.

***What's Next?*** Always try to have the prospect agree explicitly about what the next step of the relationship will be. If possible arrange to call back with more information, or to submit some paperwork for review and discussion. If the prospect isn't comfortable agreeing to a follow-up contact, they are probably not interested in your services.

## WORKSHEET: Clarify Vague Symptoms

*Often the client is not really sure what they need.  Use the following questions to help them explore their problems and possible solutions:*

1. What would you like to see improved in this situation?

2. What is it that most bothers you about the current way you're handling this situation?

3. Where are you currently spending the most time in this process?

4. What part of this process is costing the most money?

5. What do you most like about the way the current system works?

6. Does your staff share this perspective with you or do they have different concerns?

7. What makes your way of doing this different from your competitors'?  What makes your business unique?

8. If we could wave a magic wand and make one change to your business what would it be?

### ESTABLISHING THE PROSPECT'S TECHNICAL LEVEL

An important goal of your first contact with a prospect should be to determine the technical level at which that prospect functions.

If you don't do this, you are likely to annoy the prospect by overloading them with what they interpret as meaningless jargon. Or, conversely, you may insult them by talking down to them.

**GOTCHA!!**

The prospect who does not understand a word you are saying is mostly likely to signal this confusion by nodding sagely and agreeing with whatever you say. No one likes to admit they're out of their depth.

The best way to establish level is simply to ask. Don't be coy, but begin your discussion with a few questions intended to establish how much experience the person you are talking with has with computers and software and how comfortable they are with technical jargon.

Even if a prospect assures you they have a technical background, be alert for clues that they may not totally understand the technical references you have made.

### SELLING YOURSELF IN THE INTERVIEW

While you are busy trying to find out all the things you need to know, the client will, of course, be looking for the information they need to decide whether they want to work with you.

To help them make this decision you must:

- Briefly get across your strongest credential.

- Respond to their explanation of what they need done by mirroring back to them what they have told you in a way that makes it clear that you have heard and do comprehend their problems.

- Suggest that you have a solution for them without actually solving the problem on the spot for free.

- Be alert to the spoken and unspoken reservations that the client might have about your ability to do the job, and respond to these reservations with the arguments and information most likely to calm them.

## STARTING THE CLOCK

Of all of these, your biggest challenge is to avoid solving the client's problem for free. Everyone loves free advice and most people will take as much of it as they can get. But to stay in business, you need clients who are willing and able to pay for the use of your expertise.

That's why it's vital that you make sure that clients understand that you get paid for solving problems and that you expect to bill them for solving theirs. This is how professionals act, and clients will respect you more, not less, for acting as if you expect to get paid.

Here are some different ways consultants ensure that the free consultations they give quickly turn into to paying work:

- Offer a free hour to discuss the problem. Bill for any time after the hour is over.

- Offer a free initial meeting to discuss the client's problem and sketch out possible solutions. Make it clear to the prospect at the start of the meeting that this initial meeting is the only free consultation you will be giving them and that once it is over you expect to bill your time at your usual rate.

> # GOTCHA!!
>
> ### *Don't Write A Specification For Free!*
>
> The work you *do to* convince the client to hire you should never result in your giving them a piece of paper they can hand another person who can then solve the problem using the information you have provided.
>
> You'll find more discussion of specifications on Page 207.
>
>

- Meet with client and write up a free brief—and I mean *brief*—proposal offering to do a detailed study of the problem for pay.

- Offer a free "study" that will result in a written report detailing the work to be done. Make it clear that all subsequent work will be done at normal rates. This is a valid strategy only if you expect to win a large contract.

# IDENTIFYING AND RESPONDING TO THE PROSPECT'S RESERVATIONS

As a normal part of the sales process you should expect the prospect to raise objections which you must discuss and answer. To some extent, this occurs because the prospect has real reservations, but it also allows the prospect time to think over the information you've presented to them and avoid making any premature commitments.

Before you meet with prospects you might want to review the following list of common reservations prospects are likely to express, and the range of responses available to you.

## COMMON OBJECTIONS AND RESPONSES

### PROSPECT: "Your rates are so high!"

Some possible responses:

- "Because I'm an expert in this area, I get the job done much faster than others who may *seem* to charge less."

- "I think you'll find that I'm charging the same rate as other professionals who have the same credentials as I do and who do the same kind of work. In fact, my rates are on the low side."

- "Well, you know what you can afford. But I'm busy enough right now charging these rates that I must be doing something right."

- "Well, it's up to you. You might be able to cut costs by going with an inexperienced consultant. . . "

- "That's what I have to charge to stay in business."

- "You wanna bargain, go to Walmart."

### PROSPECT: "Your company is just you, right? What if you get hit by a truck?"

Some possible responses:

- "I've given some serious thought to that question because it's a valid concern to all my clients. The solution I've found is to make an arrangement with another local consultant who does this same kind of work so that we can take care of each other's clients in an emergency."

- "I've been serving some of my clients for over six years, and I'm still very much in business—which is more than you can say for a lot of much larger companies. Size is no guarantee in this business, in fact, a company like mine that does only one thing—supporting clients like you—is much less likely to change its strategic direction than a larger company."

- "What if *you* get hit by a truck?"

### PROSPECT: "Well, I don't know. Here you're suggesting that I buy a custom system, when my brother-in-law says I can do everything I need to do with a few Lotus 1-2-3 macros."

Some possible responses:

- "I can only tell you what I'd recommend. But I don't think you'd have called me in here if you'd really believed that a satisfactory solution was that easy."

- "Well, feel free to call me if that solution doesn't work out."

- "Yeah," <laughing> "I have a brother-in-law like that too."

### PROSPECT: "I see this is your first venture into consulting. What makes you think you can do the job?"

Some possible responses:

- "While I'm new to consulting, I've been solving precisely this kind of problem for the past five years in my job as a [your credential goes here]."

- "That's a good question and you're wise to ask. I've brought along a list of some people I've done work for in the past. Please feel free to call any of them and ask them what kind of a job you can expect me to do for you."

- "I figured you'd ask that question, so I brought along my laptop. Would you like me to show you a demo of a some software I developed on my own using the same technology I'd be offering you? Seeing it in action should give you a much better idea of what kind of results I produce than anything I could say."

- "What makes me think I can do the job? <smiling> Optimism. But I don't think you would have invited me here today if you didn't think I had what it takes to solve your problem."

---

## SOAP BOX

### *"Hmmm. I Dunno. . ."*

Write a list of three reservations which a prospect might have about hiring you.

Give a brief speech answering each one.

---

## DO YOU REALLY NEED THIS CLIENT?

All experienced consultants know that there are clients you are better off *not* working for. If you're lucky, you'll be able to identify them at the interview—before they've had a chance to sink their fangs into you. If not, you may end up deeply regretting landing that job you were so excited about getting.

There's no proven method guaranteed to identify all bad-news clients, but there are some warning signals that almost always flag trouble ahead.

Read through the following list of things prospects tell consultants, and see if you can explain why each speaker may well be—

## ☠ **THE CLIENT FROM HELL** ☠

☠ "We got badly ripped off by the last consultant we worked with. Would you believe, he wanted to charge us for support calls after the system was installed!"

☠ "Our previous developer left the project about 95% complete. All you've got to do is to tie up a few loose ends."

☠ "It doesn't matter that you've never worked on a process control system before. You look like a real smart guy. I'm sure you can do whatever needs to be done."

☠ "I see you recommended that we use a bifurcated framis. Well, I think bifurcated framises stink. And don't think you can pawn off some obsolete gecklers on us either. I read the trade magazines and I know what's what."

☠ "I don't have the details worked out yet, but I need you to give me a solid estimate of what it's going to cost to do this job so I can get the project approved before we go any further."

☠ "As I see it, this is a great opportunity for both of us. After you design the software for us [or write the book, or design the training program] our company will sell it to hundreds of other small companies just like us. Of course, because of our heavy start-up costs, we won't be able pay you for the development work, but we will give you a royalty on every copy sold. You'll make a fortune."

☠ "I'm sorry but it's our company policy never to pay in advance for services. If you can't trust us to pay you a lump sum payment after you've finished installing the system, I'm not sure we can do business together."

☠ "There's no need for a contract. I trust you."

## THE KEY TO UNDERSTANDING THE CLIENT FROM HELL

The client who has been "ripped off" by another consultant, may have, in fact, been ripped off. But it's just as likely that they had unreasonable expectations or that they define a satisfactory business relationship as one in which they get everything they want for free.

If the previous consultant wasn't run over by the proverbial truck, it is highly unlikely that he left any project "95% complete." You can bet good money that this project either needs to be redone from scratch, or that management needs a scapegoat to blame when they cancel it.

Be especially wary of the client who doesn't seem to care about your ability to do the job and who will seemingly hire any warm body. He's probably looking for a scapegoat.

The client who insists on making it clear he knows more about everything than you do is, at best, no fun to work for. At worst, he'll refuse to pay because "I could have done twice as good a job on my own in half the time."

Never let the client lure you into giving anything that might turn into a firm price quote for an undefined project!

Don't develop custom software for a client in return for nothing but royalties on future sales. You are unlikely to see these largely imaginary royalties. The client who makes such an offer is almost certainly trying to con you into working for free. If a client isn't willing to pay you a nonrefundable advance on royatlies equal to what you'd earn writing the code at your usual hourly rate, you can be sure that their real expectation of what the software will earn is less rosy than the picture they've painted for you.

If you want to bet on uncertainties, go to the race track. It's foolish to gamble on whether or not you'll ever see a dime for your work. If you don't get paid until the project is complete, there's a good chance you may never get paid at all.

A contract is there to protect *you*, not just the client. If you work without one you may have great trouble being paid, or may find the client claiming that you agreed to terms you had no intention of agreeing to.

## SOAP BOX

### *"Thanks, But No Thanks"*

Prepare a polite statement explaining why you have to decline the opportunity to work for a client.

You may cite the actual reason, for example, "I don't think we can work together right now with you being so unhappy about my rate" or you can use a polite excuse such as "I'm afraid that since we last discussed your project, I've gotten booked up." This last response is a good way to sidestep an unsolvable problem like the client's personality.

## DO YOU NEED A FORMAL PROPOSAL?

You don't want to do more unpaid work than you have to, so don't volunteer to write a formal proposal unless the client specifically requests one. All you may need to do is send the client is a brief letter recapitulating the client's problems and describing how you intend to solve them.

If a proposal *is* requested, be careful! It is all too easy to deliver a document that shows the prospect how to solve the problem without your help. That kind of document is called a "Specification" and it is a deliverable for which you should get paid. A proposal, in contrast, should get across that you understand

### GOTCHA!!

When you meet with a prospect, handle any interruptions from existing clients with great care. Prospects will be watching how you react to your beeper and handle your other clients on the phone to gauge how you might treat them.

the problem and have a solution, but not present the solution itself in detail. Use the chart on the next page to distinguish between a *proposal*—a sales document you prepare for free, and a *specification*, a design document for which you should be paid.

**Table 8. Proposal Vs Specification**

| Proposal | Specification |
|---|---|
| A selling tool | A design document |
| Sketch | Blueprint |
| Describes general approach to solving problem | Describes details of how the problem will be solved |
| Written to sell one consultant's ability to solve the problem | Can be used by anyone to solve the problem |
| Is based on what the prospect tells you in the interview | Is based on information derived from extensive interviewing and research |
| May define a specification as a deliverable | Is a deliverable |
| Usually provided for free as as part of the sales process | Usually done for compensation |

# PROPOSAL WORKSHEET

*Use the following worksheet to develop an effective proposal.*

1.  What exactly is the problem to be solved?

2.  What approach will you take to solving the problem?

3.  What will you accomplish? Do not go into *how!*

4.  Why will you take this approach?

5.  What are the benefits to the client of solving the problem this way?

6.  What work that may have been discussed will NOT be included in the project?

7.  Why should you, rather than someone else, solve this problem?

8.  When will work begin and how long is it estimated to take?

9.  What will you charge for the work? Give a ballpark estimate for the total cost of the project based on your current understanding of it.

10.  What will be the agreed upon procedure for payment?

## WHEN THE CLIENT INSISTS ON A SPECIFICATION

If the client insists on getting a detailed specification before they'll commit to a project, here are some approaches you can take to handle the situation:

- *Offer to write the specification for a fixed fee.* Some consultants do specifications at a price considerably less than what they usually charge for their time in the belief that the client who is willing to pay anything for the specification is showing that they are serious about solving the problem. Others write the specification at their usual rate, explaining that the specification will be written in such a way that it will allow anyone—not just the author, to do the job.

> ## GOTCHA!!
>
> In some states, including California, a proposal that includes a detailed description of deliverables and a price may be interpreted by the courts as a legal contract.
>
>

- *Explain why you have to charge for a detailed specification.* Explain that working without a detailed spec is like framing a building before you've decided how big to make the rooms, and that accepting a canned solution may mean ending up with a solution that only approximates your needs. Conclude by explaining that designing a system that does exactly what you want takes enough upfront design work that no serious professional can afford to do it for free.

- *Don't write a true specification. Write a proposal.* Suggest that you can solve the problem without giving away the details of how. If the client cannot understand your desire to get paid for your work, they are not a client you want to work for.

- *Remind the client of TINSTAAFL.* Point out that competing consulting houses who offer supposedly free detailed specifications are almost certainly using canned specs to sell a pre-packaged solution, and that any such specification is not going to embody detailed analysis of the client's actual situation and needs.

## Example 7.  Sample Proposal

PHARMACY SYSTEMS
123 Mattoon Street,
Springfield MA  12345
24 Hour Toll Free Support Line  1-800-527-4167

April 23, 1995

PROPOSAL
LEGAL DRUG COMPANY CUSTOMER INFORMATION AND MARKETING SYSTEM

Objective: Develop, install, and maintain a flexible new customer
information database that will improve Legal Drug's customer
service capabilities and use the information collected about
clients as a powerful marketing tool.

WHY DEVELOP A NEW SYSTEM?

Legal Drug's existing system tracks insurance claims and flags
possible drug interaction problems. It generates invoices for
insurers, customer receipts, and accounting reports. The system
was supplied by a vendor who is no longer in business and there is
no way to modify the reports it prints or to access the data it
collects with new reporting programs.

Competing pharmacies use systems that print custom messages and
informational extracts from the PDR on customer receipts. Legal
Drugs wants to offer its clients a level of service above and
beyond what its competitors can offer.

HIGHLIGHTS OF THE NEW SYSTEM:

The new system will generate reports almost identical to the ones
the old system provided to maintain continuity in operations.
In addition, new features will enable Legal Drugs to automatically
generate letters.

These letters may inform customers when their insurance plans have changed coverage, when they need to review their prescriptions with a doctor, when a new drug has come out that may be an improvement on their current medication, and when their patronage of Legal Drugs entitles them to take advantage of specials available only to steady customers.

The system will allow for the printing of PDR information as well as a changing marketing message on customer receipts, tailored to the customers' specific prescriptions.

The system will collect and report on demographic information about clients that will allow Legal Drugs to fine tune its newspaper advertising and direct mail campaigns. It will also track patterns of demand for pharmaceutical products by Legal Drugs' clients and allow for more precise ordering.

The system will be installed on Legal Drug's existing computers (Networked Acer 486 DX-33s). It will require investment in new point-of-sale printers capable of supplying the new, enhanced, customer printouts. No additional hardware is needed.

The developers will not modify or replace Legal Drug's bookkeeping software, also provided by their old vendor, as it is a stand-alone product not connected with the customer information system.

WHY USE PHARMACY SYSTEMS AS YOUR SOFTWARE DEVELOPER?

Pharmacy Systems has been providing systems to pharmacies since 1984. Not only are we specialists in pharmacy systems, we sell service, and support nothing but pharmacy systems. This demonstrates a commitment to our pharmacy customers no competitor can match.

The principals of Pharmacy Systems are Esther Hodges, Reg. Ph. and Tom Hodges, who joined us after having been Manager of Customer Software Development at the corporate headquarters of Big Time Drugs.

To date, Pharmacy Systems has installed 45 pharmacy systems throughout the United States. While we continue to refine and improve our systems, our ability to reuse much of the existing code from previously developed system allows us to provide custom systems at a near off-the-shelf price.


PROJECT SPECIFICS:


Work can begin within three weeks of the signing of a contract. It is estimated that it will take three months to install and test the complete system.

It is estimated, based on our experience with other pharmacy clients, that the cost of the completed system should not exceed $6,000. However, a more detailed estimate can be presented only after a formal, detailed specification is delivered by Pharmacy Systems and accepted by Legal Drug. Pharmacy Systems will provide such a detailed specification to Legal Drugs for a fee of $500, one half of which is to be paid before the work commences. Development of the rest of the system will be reimbursed at Pharmacy System's regular hourly rate of $50/hr., billed monthly. Pharmacy system will also provide a one-day training class for Legal Drug's employees at a total cost of $400 which includes training materials.

After the installation of the new system, Pharmacy Systems will provide one year of free on-site service to correct any defects in the system which fail to match the detailed specification agreed upon between Pharmacy Systems and Legal Drugs.

Please feel free to contact Esther Hodges at Pharmacy Systems on our 24-hour toll free number at 1-800-123-4567 if you have any questions about this proposal or require further information.

## SAMPLE SPECIFICATION

The following represents an excerpt of the detailed specification which would describe the pharmacy system proposed above. This section describes one of the seven new reports that the new system will generate.

**Example 8. A Portion of the Project Specification**

```
CUSTOMER DEMOGRAPHICS REPORT.
Input 1:  Customer Identification Record
Field Name                          Length/type
Zip Code                            9 alphanumeric
Doctor Code                         4 alphanumeric from
                                    Doctor file,
Insurer Code                        3 alphanumeric from
                                    Insurer File
Referred By                         25 alphanumeric


Input 2:  Customer Visit Record
Fields Processed                    Length
Purchase Amount/Visit               5 dollar numeric
Special Offers Made Code            3 alphanumeric from
                                    Premium File
Special Offers Taken Code           3 alphanumeric from
                                    Premium File


Report Frequency:  Monthly. Manual Override? Y.
Launched From:
  a.      Monthly Automatic Report Generation (Menu M03)
  b.      Visit Report Selection Menu (Menu V01).


Report Output:
  a.      Total Customer Purchases Sorted By Zip Code.
          Change In Purchase Totals By Zip Code From Previous
          Reporting Period.
  b.      Total Customer Purchases Sorted By Insurance Plan.
          Change In Purchase Totals By Insurance Plan From Previous
          Reporting Period.
  c.      Total Customer Purchases Sorted By Doctor/Practice/HMO
          Change In Purchase Totals By Doctor From Previous
          Reporting Period.
  d.      Total Customer Purchases Sorted By Referral Source.
          Change In Purchase Totals By Referral Source From
          Previous Reporting Period.
```

## AFTER THE FIRST MEETING

You may be offered an assignment during the first meeting. If this occurs, it is a good idea to respond in writing immediately after your meeting. Send the client a polite letter that recapitulates all the significant points you've discussed about what the project will consist of, how you'll be paid, and when you'll begin. This will ensure that you have been accurate in your assessment of what you and the client agreed to in the meeting.

However, in many cases you must take several more steps before you get to a commitment. If the prospect shows interest but your first interview is not conclusive, do the following:

- Send additional written or printed information and call to discuss it.

- Send a polite letter briefly recapitulating the client's problem and sketching out a solution. Call after it should have been received and ask if the prospect has any further questions.

- Offer to provide site visits to satisfied clients or on-site demos.

- Call back and ask when a decision can be expected.

- If you've agreed to present a formal proposal, present it, and then call back to ask if there are any questions you can answer.

- When the client's questions are answered and you've provided a reasonable amount of time for consideration, ask for the sale.

## SOAP BOX

Tape your first meeting with a client. Refer to it after you complete a project for that same client.

- What questions do you now wish you had asked at that interview that you didn't?

- What important issues did you misunderstand or miss entirely?

- Did you waste time on what now seem to have been irrelevant topics?

- How well did you gauge the client's personality, needs, and technical level?

## A SAMPLE SALES PROCESS

The following example is intended to give you a feeling for how the consultant can best manage the delicate process of getting from the initial interview to a signed contract.

The consultant has been discussing the client's problems with an outdated bookkeeping system that can't handle international transactions. Here's how she wraps up the meeting:

| | |
|---|---|
| *CONSULTANT*: | *Thank you for taking the time to explain that to me. I think by now that I've got a good grasp of your problem with currency conversions. Let me get back to you with that article from* PC World *we mentioned that compared the top off-the-shelf solutions. I think you'll find it revealing. Then after you've had a chance to review it, I'll call you back to see if you want to go that route or whether you'd like me to set up a demo of our custom bookkeeping system for you.* |

The consultant mails the article along with the letter on Page 217.

Four days after mailing this letter, if the client has not called back, it would be appropriate to call back:

| | |
|---|---|
| *CONSULTANT*: | *Hi, this is Anna Taylor from InterNatAccount. Did you get a chance to review the material I sent you?* |
| *CLIENT*: | *Yes. Thanks.* |
| *CONSULTANT*: | *So what are you thinking now about the direction you'd like to take?* |
| *CLIENT*: | *Well, I think we do need a custom solution of some sort, but it's hard to know exactly what to do . . ..* |
| *CONSULTANT*: | *Would you like me to set up that demo for you? It will only take half an hour and I think it will answer a lot of your questions.* |

At this point if the client agrees, the consultant will set up an appointment.

## Example 9.  First Meeting Follow-up Letter

```
                        InterNatAccount
                1330 Prestige Park, Suite 330
                      Hurst, TX   71318


September 25, 1995


Edward Abercrombie, President
Baskets Unlimited
23481 Sotogrande Rd
Grand Prairie, TX   71368



Dear Mr. Abercrombie,

I greatly enjoyed our meeting last week. Here's the article I promised
you. I think you're right to consider a custom solution in your
situation, since, as you can see, none of these shrink-wrapped products
is going to track your overseas sales and currency conversions and
treat them the way you want to have them treated for your reporting
needs.

I understand your concern about the expense of a custom system, but I
think that after you see our demo you'll realize how closely our base
system already fits your needs, and how little actual custom work is
needed to adapt it to your unique requirements. We've specialized for
over five years in providing accounting packages for companies doing
business overseas so we've had a lot of experience solving the same
kinds of problems you are encountering now.

If you'd like any further information about this material, or about our
custom systems for international accounting needs, please don't
hesitate to call me at 209-973-8831.

Yours truly,


Anna Taylor
```

After the demo and a discussion in which the client and consultant discuss the scope and expense of the project, the following would be appropriate:

| | |
|---|---|
| **CONSULTANT:** | *Do you have any other questions I could answer?* |
| **CLIENT:** | *No, I think we've got all the information we need.* |
| **CONSULTANT:** | *Great. Would you like us to provide a system for you?* |

If the client agrees, the consultant should mail out a simple letter of agreement like the one shown on Page 219, and then present the client with a formal contract.

If the client does not give immediate approval, a reply along the lines of the following is appropriate:

| | |
|---|---|
| **CONSULTANT:** | *When do you think you'll be able to make a firm decision about whether to go ahead on this project?* |
| **CLIENT:** | *Um, well. I'm going to have to discuss it with a few key people. It will probably take a week or two.* |
| **CONSULTANT:** | *Okay. I'll check back with you in a couple of weeks and see what you've decided. Meanwhile, if you do need any further information do give us a call.* |

Sometimes when the client stalls, it is a good idea for the consultant to probe politely for the real objection underlying the uncertainty.

| | |
|---|---|
| **CLIENT:** | *Well. . . I don't know. . .* |
| **CONSULTANT:** | *What seems to be your biggest concern right now?* |
| **CLIENT:** | *The cost. I don't think we've got the budget to handle a full custom treatment.* |
| **CONSULTANT** | *Well, that's possible. <pause> But we did discuss your budget for the project last week, and the figure you gave me is more than enough to cover the solution we could provide for you. Because we reuse so much code from our previous projects we don't have to reinvent the wheel every time we create a custom solution.* |

## Example 10.  Letter of Agreement

InterNatAccount
1330 Prestige Park, Suite 330
Hurst, TX   71318

September 25, 1995

Edward Abercrombie, President
Baskets Unlimited
23481 Sotogrande Rd
Grand Prairie, TX   71368

Dear Mr. Abercrombie,

This is to confirm that we will be providing you with an
InterNatAccount bookkeeping system.  This system will consist of a
modification of our baseline InterBook System with the floating
currency modifications described in our memo dated June 2, 1995.

As we discussed, we will be discounting our usual rate of $75/hr, to
$65/hr as a result of your willingness to sign up for our Preferred
Customer Support program.  All hours spent by InterNatAccount and its
subcontractors on this project will be billed at this rate.

We estimate that the project will require four weeks of full-time work
by one of our consultants.  We will be furnishing a formal project
specification as the first phase of this project.  Please make sure
that you and your staff review this document fully and carefully before
you approve it, as all further work on your system will be based on
this important design document.

You will be receiving the formal contract we discussed by next week.
Work will begin on the project on acceptance of the signed contract.

If you have any further questions, please feel free to contact me at
209 973-8831.

Sincerely,

Anna Taylor

At this point the consultant may probe for further objections, or, if she can't identify the objection, may simply end the conversation with a further promise of follow-up.

| | |
|---|---|
| **CLIENT:** | *Let me think about this for a while and then get back to you on it.* |
| **CONSULTANT:** | *Fine! And if you come up with any further thoughts, or questions give me a call.* |

One last follow-up call a few weeks later to touch base and inquire if the client has made any further decisions about the direction they plan to take in solving their bookkeeping problems later would be appropriate. However, if the client does not show signs of wanting to move the project forward, there's no point in harassing them.

## COMMENTS ON THE SAMPLE SALES PROCESS

- Use your follow up material to address any client reservations— both those they've expressed out loud and those you suspect they're harboring.

- Once you've presented a proposal—formal or informal, answered the client's questions and addressed their concerns, don't dodge the issue: *ask for the sale.*

- If the client won't or can't commit when you ask for the sale, you have a right to ask them when they do expect to make their decision.

- You can never know what the real reasons are for a client's postponing a decision. Never assume that no decision means a "no" decision. But if you've given it your best shot and the client leaves you hanging, hope for the best and put your energy into marketing yourself elsewhere.

- If a client rejects your proposal or hires someone else, it is appropriate to politely ask them why. The answer you get may help you win your next contract.

# 7 NEGOTIATE YOUR INDEPENDENT CONSULTING CONTRACT

**CHAPTER OBJECTIVE**

**Use contract negotiations to solve business problems before they start**

- Understand how negotiating a contract helps you avoid future problems

- Master the fundamentals of negotiation

- Learn what contract clauses mean and which ones are worth fighting for

- Find out how to deal with sticky negotiating points

When a client asks you to do a job for them, your next step should be to negotiate a formal written contract. This contract performs three vital functions:

- It ensures that you and the client are working from the same assumptions.

- It provides a clear, legally recognized record of what was agreed to.

- It forces you and the client to consider in advance how you will deal with common, easily overlooked, conflict-producing situations that might arise during the contract.

## WHO SUPPLIES THE CONTRACT

If you allow a client to have their lawyer draw up the contract for your project, you can assume that the contract's provisions will be heavily weighted in the favor of the client. This makes it worth the expense of having your own lawyer draft, or at least review, the contract for any major project you intend to pursue.

Use an attorney who specializes in computer law, or one who specializes in intellectual property law who has experience negotiating computer consulting contracts. Do *not* rely on a lawyer whose practice is mostly divorce and real estate transfers. You need someone who stays aware—on a daily basis—of the ever-changing legal issues specific to computer consulting and computer software development.

If large corporate clients insist you use their standard contracts (as often happens in contract programming situations ) you may able to negotiate terms without bringing in a lawyer. But if you have any question about the impact of a given clause, or if the client refuses to change a clause that rings warning bells after you've read the discussion of contract clauses that follows here, it is well worth paying for legal advice.

### GOTCHA!!

You can purchase software programs, such as "It's Legal" from Parsons Technology or "QuickForm Contracts" from Invisible Hand Software that provide you with blank contracts you can customize.

If you use one of these, be sure that you do not alter any of the legal wording they contain. To do so may invalidate important clauses.

# GOTCHA!!

## *WHAT CAN GO WRONG WITH A SIMPLE HANDSHAKE?*

If you are tempted to work without a contract, either because you want to avoid paying a lawyer or because you know and trust your client, consider the following:

- 💣 Your contact at a client firm may be transferred from his job or fired, leaving no one in the firm aware of what you agreed to—or willing to pay for it.

- 💣 The client may refuse to pay, claiming that you didn't do what you promised to do. It is much more difficult to prove your right to payment if it rests on an oral contract.

- 💣 The client may assume that he or she is buying services, such as lifetime support, that you did not intend to sell them. Conflicts over what you owe the client may create bad word of mouth and hamper your ability to find new clients.

- 💣 The client and consultant may make assumptions about important issues, such as who owns the rights to software developed under the contract, which are not what the law provides in the absence of a written contract.

## DON'T BE AFRAID TO NEGOTIATE

Negotiation can be a nerve-wracking experience, particularly if you are not used to doing it. But it is an essential skill all consultants must master if they are not to be taken advantage of by clients and broker firms. Use the following guidelines to stiffen your will and keep you on track when it's time to haggle over terms:

# PRINCIPLES OF NEGOTIATION

- *Before you enter negotiations, find out the range of rates, terms, and conditions usual in the situation you are negotiating and keep your demands within the limits of the possible.*

- *Decide in advance what terms and conditions you want, what terms and conditions you will settle for, and what terms and conditions are out of the question.*

- *Never accept a contract that forces you to accept a condition you've defined as unacceptable.*

- *Try to replace unacceptable conditions with compromises that you can live with.*

- *Make sure your first offer contains some fat you can cut in return for other concessions–but don't be unreasonable.*

- *Ask for at least 10% more money than you expect to get.*

- *If the client won't budge on how much they'll pay, negotiate what you will deliver for the set amount of money.*

- *If a demand is refused, don't take it personally. Keep your cool, stay friendly, and make a counteroffer.*

- *Always know what your next offer will be if this one is refused.*

- *Don't be afraid to go through two or three rounds of offer and counteroffer.*

- *Don't waste time and energy negotiating unimportant issues. Save your energy for what matters.*

- *Don't accept any offer in the heat of the moment if it involves your making significant concessions. Express interest and say, "I'll be back in touch with you as soon as I've had a chance to think this over." Then think it over.*

- *If you end up unhappy with a contract, consider it a learning experience. All beginning consultants make some contract mistakes. Your contract negotiations will become more effective as you gain more experience.*

## WHAT DOES A CONTRACT DEFINE?

While you should not try to "roll your own" contract, you do need to understand the issues addressed in a properly drawn contract, both for your own benefit and so that you can explain these issues to your client during negotiations. Here are the issues that are usually defined by computer consulting contract clauses:

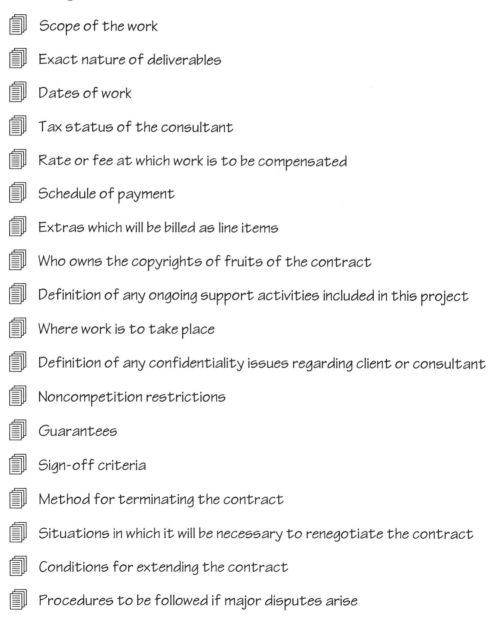

Scope of the work

Exact nature of deliverables

Dates of work

Tax status of the consultant

Rate or fee at which work is to be compensated

Schedule of payment

Extras which will be billed as line items

Who owns the copyrights of fruits of the contract

Definition of any ongoing support activities included in this project

Where work is to take place

Definition of any confidentiality issues regarding client or consultant

Noncompetition restrictions

Guarantees

Sign-off criteria

Method for terminating the contract

Situations in which it will be necessary to renegotiate the contract

Conditions for extending the contract

Procedures to be followed if major disputes arise

# CONTRACT CLAUSES AND WHAT THEY MEAN

## THE CONFIDENTIALITY/NONDISCLOSURE CLAUSE

**WHAT IT DOES:** This clause specifies what is to be considered as confidential and binds the client and/or consultant not to disclose the confidential material.

**Why You Want This Clause:** To prevent the client from giving your specifications, code, or proprietary libraries to a competitor.

**Why Clients Want This Clause:** To prevent you from revealing information about a new product, method, marketing plan, or company strategy to a competitor, the press, or the general public.

**WHAT TO WATCH OUT FOR:** Overly broad wording that limits your ability to work for competitors. Overly broad definition of confidential material. Wording that keeps you from reusing generic code for new clients. Lack of clarity about when the period of confidentiality ends.

## THE NONCOMPETITION CLAUSE

**WHAT IT DOES:** Limits you from working for certain types of clients for a period of time after you end a contract. This noncompetition clause is not the same as the broker noncompetition clauses you'll find discussed in Chapter Five which oblige you to work through a given broker firm. This clause's intent is usually to keep you from working for the client's competitors.

**Why You Want This Clause:** You don't.

**Why Clients Want This Clause:** To keep you from giving a competitor the benefit of systems they've paid you to develop or install.

**WHAT TO WATCH OUT FOR:** Overly restrictive clauses that prevent you from working in entire industries or writing any systems of the type you developed for the client. Clauses that do not specify the end date of the noncompetition period or which specify one longer than a year.

## OWNERSHIP OF THE FRUITS OF THE CONTRACT

**WHAT IT DOES:** Defines who owns the copyrights to software, documents, and training programs you develop for a client.

### Why You Want This Clause:

Copyright law specifies that you, the developer, retain the copyright to anything you write as an independent contractor, unless you specifically assign it to the client. Clients don't know this and usually assume that they own the code they pay you to write for them. Specifying explicitly who owns the code avoids the misunderstandings and bad feeling that can develop around this issue.

### Why Clients Want This Clause: To clarify ownership issues.

**WHAT TO WATCH OUT FOR:** Clauses that have you signing over more than you intended.

When you develop software for a client for either a fixed or hourly rate, you need to decide whether you will give the client the rights to the software or only a license to use it.

> ### CODE OWNERSHIP
>
> In the absence of a written contract specifying otherwise, an independent contractor retains the copyright to work he or she creates under the contract.

> ### CODE OWNERSHIP OPTIONS
>
> Give the client all rights to the software and source code. This means they can resell the code or prevent you from reusing it.
>
> Give the client the the source code and the right to use and modify the source code for their own use, but reserve the right to sell it to others and to reuse it yourself.
>
> Do not give the client source code, but put that source code in escrow in case something happens to you. (See discussion, next page.)
>
> Give client the right to use the software and charge extra for the source code. Most clients will not buy the source code in this situation.
>
> Give the client the right to use the source code and negotiate for a royalty or other payment should the client resell the system to others.

## SOFTWARE ESCROW

### Q: What is Software Escrow?

**A:** The term "software escrow" refers to the situation in which you entrust software to a third party who is legally responsible for guarding it and releasing it only under certain specified conditions, for example, if you were to die and the client needed to modify your software.

### Q: Where do I find a person or organization who offers this service?

**A:** Some banks and attorneys offer this service. There are also several firms who provide software escrow services, such as Fort Knox, and Data Securities International.

### Q: How does software escrow work?

**A:** You and the client must agree on the circumstances under which the source code should be released, and to whom. Then you pay a start up fee and a separate annual fee. Software escrow is expensive and rarely makes sense unless you are dealing with a huge project and a very good reason for not turning over the code.

## TERMINATION CLAUSE

**WHAT IT DOES:** Specifies how you and/or your client can get out of the contract under certain predefined circumstances.

**Why You Want This Clause:** To take care of your responsibility should a catastrophe or illness make it impossible for you to continue work on the project.

**Why Clients Want This Clause:** To allow them to end the contract relationship should their business needs suddenly change, or should they become dissatisfied with your work.

**WHAT TO WATCH OUT FOR:** You don't want to give the client the impression that you are looking for loopholes or will abandon them if a better opportunity arises—or if you get offered a full time job. So write this clause to refer specifically to extraordinary circumstances or, match the wording that the client demands to cover their side of the agreement.

## CONDITIONS FOR EXTENDING THE CONTRACT

**WHAT IT DOES:** In cases where you are working at an hourly rate it specifies whether the same rate (and other terms) will apply to new contracts that are made within some specified time period.

**Why You Want This Clause::** You don't

**Why Clients Want This Clause:** It protects the client against rate hikes for a specified period.

**WHAT TO WATCH OUT FOR:** These clauses are common in client-supplied contracts. If you can live with the terms they are probably not worth fighting over. In practice you are not likely to raise your rates except once a year or so. However, make sure that the term you are obliged to work at the given rate is not longer than a year.

## GUARANTEE

**WHAT IT DOES:** Specifies what recourse a client has if your work doesn't live up to expectations.

**Why You Want This Clause:** You don't. But if a client demands a guarantee you should do your best to provide an acceptable one since refusing to give a guarantee is likely to lose you the client.

**Why Clients Want This Clause:** To protect against shoddy work. To protect against defective equipment. To give you an incentive to meet target deadlines.

**WHAT TO WATCH OUT FOR:** Wording that allows the client to withhold payment for software and hardware that remains in the client's possession. Penalties for problems that might arise that you have no control over—for example, late delivery of hardware from a manufacturer, or failure of a software company to release a product on its scheduled date. The requirement that you buy expensive and unnecessary insurance that costs more than you'll earn from the job. Lack of time limit on the guarantee.

## HOW TO PROVIDE FAIR GUARANTEES

Here are some ways you can design guarantees that protect your clients without setting you up for abuse:

### Stage Guarantees

Break project into steps. Specify in the contract that the "Money back guarantee" expires after the client signs off on each step. Specify sign-off criteria in writing.

### Retain Ownership

Specify in the contract that if the client exercises the right to get their money back, all rights to the deliverable you've provided revert to you and you have the right to remove it from their premises. You would also retain all rights to resell it and profit from it.

### Include Two-way Incentives

If clients insist on adding a penalty for late delivery, include a bonus for early or on-time delivery.

### Have Client Pay for Insurance

If clients insist on expensive Errors & Omissions insurance coverage ask that they pay all or a portion of the premium, since the insurance is primarily for their benefit.

## TERMS OF PAYMENT

**WHAT IT DOES:** Specifies how payment will be made and what your remedies are when the client does not pay within a specified period.

**Why You Want This Clause:** Clients who won't pay for the work for which they've contracted are a major problem for computer consultants. Use this clause to set up a payment system that gives you ample notice of payment problems and allows you to stop work on a project before you experience significant losses.

**Why Clients Want This Clause:** They don't. However, a client who will not sign a reasonable version of such a clause is NOT a client you want to do business with.

### WHAT TO WATCH OUT FOR:

Payment terms that specify that all payment is to be made after the work is complete and delivered. Payment terms that keep you from receiving a first payment until several months' worth of work is complete. Payment terms that do not allow you to stop work when a set number of invoices have gone unpaid. (See Page 104 in Chapter Three for more on payment terms.)

## ACCEPTANCE CRITERIA CLAUSE

**WHAT IT DOES:** Defines the circumstances under which the system will be certified as complete.

**Why You Want This Clause:** You want mutually agreed upon sign-off criteria to define when the product is complete. This allows you to distinguish between the project as defined in the contract and new work which requires a new contract.

> ## GOTCHA!!
> ### BEWARE OF DEADBEATS
>
> Run a credit check on any new client before you sign a contract with them. You'll be amazed how many would-be clients turn out to have rotten credit histories.
>
> You may also want to double check the creditworthiness of smaller firms by asking for the names of other local companies the firm does business with and asking if you can call them for credit references.
>
>

It also lets you distinguish between providing ongoing support (covered by a separate clause) and completing the original effort described in the contract.

**WHAT TO WATCH OUT FOR:** If you are working on a fixed rate contract, you need to have it in writing that if the client changes the specification that was the basis of your fixed rate, the rate must be renegotiated. Sign-off criteria should apply only to a system that meets your unchanged project specification.

### SAFEGUARDS AGAINST NONPAYMENT YOU CAN WRITE INTO YOUR CONTRACT

- Insist on a significant payment (30%) up front for any fixed price job.

- Keep invoicing periods short and billing amounts manageable so that payment problems become apparent before the client runs up a huge balance.

- Write into the contract that work on the project will cease if more than two invoices are open at any given time.

- Hold onto something of value until you've received the final payment.

- Offer a small discount (i.e., 2%) for payment within a short period (i.e., 30 days.) But be aware that many accounting departments will take advantage of the discount and STILL pay late.

- If you are selling merchandise in return for a series of partial payments, include the necessary legal wording in your contract to allow you to repossess if payment stops.

- If you are developing software, manuals, courses, or specifications, specify that title to these items or the copyright to these items does not pass to the client until the final payment has been made.

- If you want to be able to disable the client's deliverable by withholding something—like a software password—when nonpayment occurs, make sure that this is written into the contract and that the client explicitly approves it.

## ONGOING SUPPORT CLAUSE

**WHAT IT DOES:** Describes what support you will provide to the client after the system and/or code is delivered.

**Why You Want This Clause:** You want to distinguish between bug fixes, which you will fix for free, and enhancements and training, which you will provide at your customary rates.

**WHAT TO WATCH OUT FOR:** If training is to be included with a development project make sure that you define what constitutes training (specific classes) and that you make it clear that training does not include driving to the client's site to show staff how to use features whose use is documented in a manual and whose function has been covered in a training class.

You will also want to specify the response time that clients can expect if they call with a bug or other such problem after the project is complete.

---

### HANDLING BUGS

Every new system has bugs. Make life easy on yourself and your clients by doing the following:

- Agree beforehand on clear-cut criteria for declaring the system complete. Make sure that the client understands that adding new features requires renegotiation of acceptance criteria.

- Explain that there will be a shakeout period after the software is first installed when problems may emerge. Get across that this is a normal part of the development cycle, not a sign you've done a poor job.

- Assure clients that any bugs emerging within the first weeks of installation will be given priority response— immediate if possible. Allow for a longer response to problems that emerge once the system is stable.

- Make sure that the client understands that you will charge for ongoing support once the system is stable.

234 of 286 The Computer Consultant's Workbook

## SETTLING DISPUTES

**WHAT IT DOES:** Describes a mechanism for settling serious disputes. Options include calling on the services of an arbitrator, or specifying who pays for a successful lawsuit.

**Why You Want This Clause:** If you can agree to use a formal arbitrator you may be able to resolve serious disputes much more cheaply and in a more timely manner.

**Why Clients Want This Clause:** Same.

**WHAT TO WATCH OUT FOR:** Client-supplied wording that makes you pay for frivolous suits they bring against you.

## EXCEPTIONAL EXPENSES

**WHAT IT DOES:** Specifies that additional payment over and above your hourly rate will be made for expenses such as long distance phone calls to non-800-number vendor support numbers, long distance travel, or expensive database searches.

**Why You Want This Clause:** It is best to negotiate how such potentially hefty expense items will be handled in advance. Some consultants merely raise their rates to cover such items and do not bill for them separately. However, others prefer to break out such expenses so the client can choose whether or not to incur them.

**Why Clients Want This Clause:** Rather than pay a higher rate that reflects your expenses, the client may prefer to break them out separately and exert some control over how they are incurred. For example, a client who is paying for travel expenses may ask you to use specific vendors who offer him a discount.

**WHAT TO WATCH OUT FOR:** Unexpected expenses that cut way down on your profits. For example, parking downtown in some cities can cost as much as $60/wk. If you will be spending much time on-site for a downtown client, it may be worth negotiating for a visitor's parking permit for the company garage.

## DO NOT WORK WITHOUT A SIGNED CONTRACT

No matter what terms you may have agreed to orally, do not begin work on any assignment until you have received a signed copy of your contract. Contracts that disappear into limbo or get inexplicably hung up at the attorney's office are often a sign of the client who is playing games.

If you have reason to trust a client and do need to start work before paperwork is complete, be sure to protect yourself by mailing a letter of agreement to the client that documents the terms of the contract you expect to receive.

If your contract specifies that you should be paid a deposit or down payment before beginning work—particularly if you are ordering hardware or software for the client—do not begin work before the deposit clears.

## SOAP BOX

Prepare an answer to a client who says:

### "Why Bother with A Formal Contract?"

Stress the benefits that the client will get from going through the contract negotiation process.

---
---

# 📑 CONTRACT CHECKLIST 📑

---
---

☐ Have you defined your independent contractor status in the contract?

☐ Have you discussed ownership of the code with the client?

☐ Have you protected your tools or trade secrets?

☐ Have you provided a mechanism to amend or terminate the contract?

☐ Have you limited any guarantees?

☐ Have you defined reasonable intervals for payment?

☐ Have you defined what will happen if payment is not forthcoming?

☐ Have you defined any exceptional expenses that will be billed separately?

☐ Have you defined when the project will be considered "done?"

☐ Have you defined on-going support and distinguished it from bug fixes and new development?

☐ Have you defined the speed with which you will respond to problems?

☐ Do you have a copy of this contract signed by the client?

# 8 BE A SUCCESS ON THE JOB

**CHAPTER OBJECTIVE**

**Complete your consulting projects in a way that earns you respect, new clients, and—cash**

- Learn how to get off to a running start
- Understand the consultant mentality
- Avoid the perils that await unwary consultants
- Know the ethical guidelines all consultants should follow
- Discover how to handle mistakes you make on the job
- Learn the right way to bill
- Find out how to identify and deal with payment problems

Your new contract starts on Monday. Now you must complete the assignment in a way that creates a satisfied client. A satisfied client will praise your work and recommend your services to others, contributing to your long-term success. But if you fail to please the client, their dissatisfaction may, ruin your word of mouth, blight your reputation and contribute to the deterioration of your consulting career.

There is more to pleasing clients than just getting the job done. If you behave in a way that disturbs the client or alienates the client's employees you may complete the technical part of a contract brilliantly and still end up with a client who never calls back. By the same token, if you maintain the lines of communication throughout a crisis and behave in a way that convinces the client that you are a true professional, you may experience heart-stopping technical reverses and still end up with a client who praises you to others. Once again, the key is listening closely to the client, staying aware of the client's viewpoint and communicating with the client in a way that respects that viewpoint.

Below is a summary of what you can do to satisfy your clients. You may want to post it in a prominent place and refer to it frequently.

## HOW TO SATISFY YOUR CLIENT

- Notify the client of any steps they can take before your arrival that will let you begin work without delay.
- Take nothing for granted.
- If you don't know, ask.
- Bring your own reliable tools with you.
- Never ignore a problem or try to hide it in the hope you can pull off a last minute save.
- Communicate with your client regularly and document your progress and any emerging issues in writing.
- Always behave like a guest and not like an employee.
- Expect to find office politics everywhere and stay out of them.
- Don't mix business and romance.
- Let the client set the priorities and chose the goals.
- When forced to set your own priorities, emphasize those that match what the client considers most important.
- Let the client take credit for your achievements.

## HELP THE CLIENT PREPARE

The last thing you want to do is spend your first billable hours on an assignment sitting around waiting for someone to find you a computer, give you a password, or locate the person who is supposed to show you the problem that needs to be fixed. This is particularly true if the client is not used to working with consultants and is already anxious about having to pay on an hourly basis.

To help prevent this from happening—or at least to prevent the client from blaming you when it does—explain to the client before you arrive the steps they can take to help you be most productive. You may find it useful to provide the client with a "First Day Checklist" similar to the one displayed on Page 240.

## DEVELOP THE CONSULTING MENTALITY

If you are just starting out and are making the transition from employee to consultant, you'll also need to change the attitudes underlying the way you conduct yourself on the job.

You'll need to develop a "consulting mentality." This is a way of thinking and behaving on the job that is very different from the mindset you brought to work with you as an employee. The table on Page 241 summarizes these differences. Now we'll examine some of the issues cited in that table:

### YOUR OUTSIDER STATUS IS YOUR GREATEST STRENGTH—AND GREATEST WEAKNESS

Much of your value to the client is that you can give honest, insightful advice unhampered by intracompany politics and loyalties. But your outsider status also makes you a perfect scapegoat for management failures and an excellent lightening rod for employee anger and resentment. Should you experience either reaction, don't take them personally. They are a function of your outsider role and may well be completely unrelated to anything you have actually said or done.

Because it is the nature of consulting for you always to be the outsider wherever you may be working, your best strategy for handling the emotions this may bring up inside you is to forge close, supportive friendships with other consultants dealing with the same challenges, who can give you the friendship and support you should not expect from clients.

## Example 11. First Day Checklist

Dear Client,

I will be beginning work on your project on Thursday, March 27. To ensure that I can begin productive work immediately, saving you time and money, I suggest you ask your staff to take care of the following items before I arrive:

☐ Obtain required security clearances.

☐ Apply for any necessary company ID cards and parking stickers.

☐ If work is to be performed on-site, make sure a computer is available for my use, and check that it is connected to the appropriate network and loaded with current releases of the software you want me to work with.

☐ Provide copies of existing project specifications, documentation, and program listings, so I can familiarize myself with any work that has already been done.

☐ Provide a copy of any corporate coding or naming standards I will need to comply with in my work for you.

☐ Ask key personnel to save some time for me when they make up their schedules so that I can confer with them in a timely manner.

Thank you! I look forward to seeing you on Thursday.

Sincerely yours,


Arthur D. Goldstein

## Table 9. Employee vs. Consultant Attitudes

|  | EMPLOYEE | CONSULTANT |
|---|---|---|
| **Goal of work** | Promotion, raise | More work |
| **Length of work Relationship** | Long-term | Short-term |
| **Makes impression by** | Looking busy<br>Taking credit for success | Getting work done |
| **Status markers** | Fancy desk, corner office, etc. | None. They may offend clients |
| **Lunch talk** | Complaints about boss, job, world, etc. | Polite praise for client site or silence |
| **Appropriate people with whom to socialize** | Coworkers | Other consultants, old work buddies, friends from other companies |
| **Office politics** | Chooses sides | Remain outside of conflict |
| **Policies, Systems, etc.** | Expected to know | Ask! |
| **Strategy for handling missed deadlines** | Redefine deliverable, then declare deadline met | Ask client to advise on which course to take |
| **Technical problems** | Call on in-house help first | Call on outside help |
| **Definition of success** | Promotion to manager, raise, recognition | Staying in business five years doing what you love to do |

### THE CONSULTANT IS A GUEST

If you want to put your feet up on the furniture—do it at home. A consultant can't take the liberties an employee might take on the job.

The wise consultant will *not*:

- Complain about the quality of the food in the company cafeteria.

- Remark on the unintentional comedy content of the Corporate Human Resources video playing in the employee lounge.

- Tune the departmental radio to a political talk radio call-in show.

- Wear T-shirts containing any slogans that could possibly be construed as offensive.

- Put photos of their child or spouse on a desk assigned at a client site.
- Take a screwdriver to the overhead speaker blaring Muzak over the assigned work area.

### THE REWARDS OF CONSULTING ARE NOT THE REWARDS OF EMPLOYMENT

While the work you may do as a consultant may be very similar to what you did as an employee, the rewards you will earn from that work are entirely different. You cannot be promoted. You won't get a corner office. You won't get an award at the end of a successful project and you may not ever see a finished project again once it is complete.

The only reward you can hope for will be the money you earn and the opportunity to do more work in the future. The only way you will earn them is by satisfying your client and to do that you may have to let go of abstract concepts such as "The right way to solve the problem" and replace them with concrete ones like, "The solution the client wants."

## ETHICAL CONSIDERATIONS

Inevitably, you will find yourself in situations in which what the client wants is *not* something you can go along with. In this situation, you must remember another important consulting principle:

### YOUR ULTIMATE RESPONSIBILITY IS TO YOURSELF AND YOUR BUSINESS

Serving the interests of the client should never involve violating your own moral code or personal integrity.

If you feel that a client is making a serious mistake it is appropriate to raise the issue with the client—politely. But if the client is not swayed by your arguments and wants you to implement a solution you feel is misguided, you may have to dissociate yourself from the client and their project rather than have your name and reputation be linked with a potentially disastrous outcome.

Besides the situation in which a client may want you to do what you know is wrong, there are several other ethical issues of importance to consultants that you should be aware of. Familiarize yourself with the principles on the next page and adhere to them at all times:

## GUIDELINES FOR ETHICAL BEHAVIOR

- Never take a commission from a vendor on a product that a client has paid you to recommend.

- Never violate client confidentiality.

- Disclose any conflicts of interest that come up while working for a client—in particular, any connections you have with a client's competitors or any financial stake you have in any company with which the client may do business.

- Do not recruit client employees to work for yourself or any other company.

- Do not accept work you are not competent to perform.

- Do not work while your judgment is impaired by illness, drugs, or alcohol.

- Do not turn a blind eye when a client is violating the law. This includes the use of pirated software.

## DEVELOP A HEALTHY PARANOIA

The essence of consulting is that you continually find yourself in new situations in which you cannot possibly know what is going on. This makes it essential that you fight against the normal human tendency fit into a new situation by acting as if you belong there. You don't, and unless you keep this truth in mind, you're going to get badly bitten by the many things in each new environment that you don't know about and need to find out about fast.

To illustrate the shift in attitude that you must make, consider what you would do in the following situation: You've fully tested some software on your computer and it runs flawlessly, but when you install it on the client's machine it crashes every time you try to access a record. What would you do next?

If you'd assume that you'd missed something in your testing and start tearing apart your code, you are not thinking like a consultant. A consultant's first move would be to check that there wasn't a pre-existing problem with the client's system. They'd deinstall their code and check whether other software could access the files they were trying to read. They'd ask questions like: Is the release of the database system the same as the one they were told to use? Is the virus checker on the system up-to-date and has it been run recently? How is memory allocated? Only when they were sure that the client's system was working properly would they start debugging their code.

A consultant should never assume that a client's systems and software are installed properly or that the client's staff know what they are doing. A consultant should never assume that their clearest explanations have been understood or their direst warnings heeded. In short, they should never assume anything!

If you take this approach, you may often be pleasantly surprised—clients will frequently do things right and will often have much to teach you. But by taking it you also won't end up the victim of other people's incompetence in the many cases where your paranoia is completely justified.

## REAL CONSULTANTS ASK LOTS OF QUESTIONS

Because it is impossible for any person to come into a new work environment and know everything there is to know, good consultants ask lots of questions as part of orienting themselves to a new assignment.

Obviously, the questions you ask should not be ones like "What is DOS?" But you should feel free to ask the following:

## LEGITIMATE QUESTIONS YOU CAN AND MUST ASK

- How is the data stored on this system?

- How is the system backed up and how often?

- Who is responsible for doing this task?

- Who in the company knows the most about the company's systems and how they interact?

- Whom should you call for tech support problems?

- Who will be using the system you are designing? Does the person who hired you want you to interact with that person directly or not?

- What are the procedures for moving software into formal testing? Into production? Is there a special test system?

- Who else, besides you, has access to the test data/test platform? When you run a test, are you going to be picking up other people's test modules?

- Is there some boilerplate that people in this company use when writing new code?

- Does the client have a set of utilities they prefer you to use?

- Does the client have home-brewed systems software, operating system extensions, or utilities you ought to know about?

- Does the client mind if you run your own utilities on their systems?

- Is there anything unusual about the way they've installed some standard product?

- How does the company like its systems documented? Is there a skeleton used in the company for writing documentation?

- Is there a vendor the company prefers for hardware or software purchases and/or support? Is there a reason that you should use this vendor when buying for them?

- What is the history of the project you are working on?

- In addition, if you find yourself in a situation where something just plain doesn't make sense, or where something that ought to work won't work, feel free to ask if there's something specific you ought to know about the software or hardware. Every company has its own way of doing things, and this often extends to making peculiar custom modifications to software and even hardware.

## EVERYONE MAKES MISTAKES—EVEN CONSULTANTS

You may be an expert, but you are still mortal. This means you are going to screw up occasionally, and occasionally screw up badly.

What distinguishes the pros from the amateurs is not that the pros don't make mistakes—it's what they do after they realize they've made a mistake.

### HANDLE MISTAKES LIKE A PRO

- Take responsibility even if others may have contributed to the situation.

- Never try to cover up a problem, but take immediate steps to correct it as soon as you become aware that a problem exists.

- Call on a network of other professionals for guidance and expert help appropriate to the situation.

- When the problem cannot be cleared up immediately, notify the client or the client's representative that a problem has developed and allow them to have input into the decision as to how to approach the problem.

- Don't charge clients for fixing a problem you created or for cleaning up after an error you committed when the problem or error results from your own incompetence.

### SHOULD YOU CHARGE FOR FIXING YOUR OWN MISTAKES?

New consultants often have trouble knowing when it is appropriate to charge for the work they put into fixing a problem that emerges while they're working on a project. One useful guideline to follow is this: ask yourself if the problem is one that arises out of the nature of the work—in which case you can feel comfortable charging to repair it, or whether it was due to your own incompetence.

For example, if you discover that your code can't run in the client's system because of a conflict caused by a nonstandard driver supplied with the client's cheap mail order clone video board you can confidently charge for the time it takes you to track down and solve the problem. That is because the problem you are faced with here is one that could easily confound many other computer professionals were they to attempt to do similar work for the client.

However, if you accidentally erase the client's accounting records and then discover that there is no backup file, you should immediately volunteer to do whatever it takes to right the situation for free, since your error was one of incompetence. Sometimes it is not easy to draw the line. You can use the worksheet you'll find on the next page to help you assess whether or not to charge for an error that you make on the job.

## WORKSHEET: Should You Charge For Correcting The Error?

1. Did it take more than an hour of your time to correct the error?

2. Did the error cause you, the client, or the client's employees to lose or have to redo valuable work?

3. Was this an error other people with your own skill level might be expected to make?

4. Were you aware when you made the error that you were in a situation where such an error was possible?

5. Is the problem the result of a hardware or software incompatibility that is not generally known?

6. Were you working with bleeding edge technology when you encountered difficulty?

7. Did you warn the client that this kind of problem might occur before taking the action that caused the problem?

## SCORING THE WORKSHEET:

If you answered "Yes" to questions 1 or 2 and "No" to more than three of questions 3 through 7, you have probably made an error which the client is likely to perceive as an important one, and one that was caused by your own incompetence. In such a case, the best policy is to offer to fix the problem for free.

If you answered "No" to questions 1 and 2, and "Yes" to more than one of the next questions, the error only cost a small amount of time, is not likely to upset the client, and can be treated as a normal part of getting the job done.

If you answered "Yes" to questions 4 through 6 and "No" to question 7, you need to be let new clients know that oddball, frustrating errors come with the territory when you work with bleeding edge technology, and that they should expect to pay you for the time it takes to clear up such problems.

## WATCH OUT FOR OFFICE POLITICS

The only thing you can know about the internal politics of any project you join is that there are going to be some. But your strength as a consultant derives from being perceived as being an outsider with no stake in local political struggles.

The longer the time you spend on any project, and the more closely you work with a client, the more likely you are to get sucked into political struggles that may compromise your objectivity. Be alert to the warning signs that this might be happening. Use the following questionnaire to test how well you're doing:

## WORKSHEET: Are You Getting Sucked In?

1. Do you respond emotionally to client personnel?
   ☐ Yes  ☐ No

2. Do you have personal conversations with client personnel at lunch?
   ☐ Yes  ☐ No

3. Have you begun responding to the client who hired you as an authority figure (i.e., boss) instead of as an equal who is paying you for services?
   ☐ Yes  ☐ No

4. Are you upset because the large project you are involved in is not going well even when the problems are clearly caused by client personnel or other consultants and no one is blaming you?
   ☐ Yes  ☐ No

5. Have you gotten sloppy about attending functions at which you can network and pursue your own business's marketing efforts?
   ☐ Yes  ☐ No

6. Do you find yourself getting upset about the location of an office you've been given at the client site or about an after work invitation you've been left out of?
   ☐ Yes  ☐ No

7. Has the client offered you a full time job and are you tempted to take it?
   ☐ Yes  ☐ No

If you answered "Yes" to *any* of the questions above there is a very good chance that you are getting sucked in!

# THE PERILS OF LONG-TERM CONTRACTS FOR CONTRACT PROGRAMMERS

It is particularly easy to get sucked into an employee-like state of mind when you are a contract programmer who works on-site for extended periods of time. If that is your situation, you'll have to make an extra effort to remind yourself that you really work for yourself and that your current contract is just one of many temporary work situations.

Keep in mind these reasons why working extended contracts as a contract programmer can be dangerous to your long-term consulting success.

### THE DANGERS OF OVERLONG CONTRACTS

❧ ***You become dependent on a single client for work.***
Try to cycle through a variety of client shops, never staying more than six or at most nine months at a single site, so that you build up a network of satisfied clients that can bring you new work when you need it.

❧ ***Your skills get stagnant and you miss out on learning new technologies.***
When you work for one client for an extended period, you will only get on-the-job exposure to the software that client has installed. This can render your skills too client-specific and cause you to lose touch with the directions other clients are taking in developing technological solutions.

❧ ***You become tied to one broker psychologically and legally.***
If you work short contracts through a variety of brokers, they will all be likely to keep you in mind for new contracts. But if you work for one broker for an extended period, the others will put you into their "inactive" files. You may also become lazy in your marketing efforts since you are busy and there is no end in sight to your current contract. When you are ready for a new assignment, your contacts may have evaporated and you may be forced to take whatever job your old broker can find for you, on whatever terms they offer, or you may find yourself bound by old noncompetition clauses that force you to keep working for that same broker.

# WATCH YOUR LANGUAGE

Consultants often annoy their clients by using phrases that are common in the computer community but have different meanings to people outside that community. Here are two examples of phrases that might cause trouble:

**CONSULTANT** (responding to the client's voicing of a concern): "That's trivial."

**WHAT THE CONSULTANT MEANS TO COMMUNICATE:** "Relax. My technical analysis suggests that this is not a problem that is going to blow us out of the water."

**WHAT THE CLIENT HEARS:** "You're making a big deal out of nothing. You're concerned with unimportant trivia."

**CONSULTANT** (Responding to a client's description of a possible problem): "That's a nit."

**WHAT THE CONSULTANT MEANS TO COMMUNICATE:** "This is very easily taken care of."

**WHAT THE CLIENT HEARS:** "You're making a big deal out of nothing." or "You're a nitwit."

## DON'T MIX BUSINESS WITH PLEASURE

Dating clients or client employees is a sure way to ruin even the most promising business relationship. At best, you run the risk of being accused of getting work through the consulting equivalent of the casting couch. At worst, a dating relationship turned rancid may do more to poison your company's "word of mouth" than if you broke a dozen computers.

Here are just a few of the scenarios that can occur when you date a client or client employee:

💣 You both fall madly in love. You try to hide it but, of course, someone catches you kissing in the parking lot. Result: Client's employees begin to hint that you got the contract for talents unrelated to your computer abilities. You find it much harder to get their cooperation.

💣 In companies with explicit policies about nepotism (hiring family members or other significant others) your relationship will be considered grounds for replacing you with another consultant—or firing the client employee.

💣 You do not fall madly in love, but the client or employee falls madly in love with you. Result: It becomes extremely uncomfortable to visit the client's offices or call them. The client or client employee corners you when you visit and dissolves into floods of tears or angry recriminations. If this happens, the chances are good that you've just lost a client.

💣 You both fall madly in love for a while, then you change your mind. Result: Hell hath no fury like a client scorned. You'll be lucky to get out of this one without a lawsuit.

💣 You fall madly in love but the client or client employee does not. Result: You can't get your calls answered. If you keep calling you may be accused (possibly with reason) of sexual harassment. The client tells his or her friends hilarious stories about the sex-crazed consultant they brought in. You start getting anonymous phone calls full of giggles and heavy breathing on your business line.

## MAKE SURE YOU GET PAID

Up until now, we've been focusing on how to succeed on the job, but that success can feel pretty hollow if you don't get paid for the work that you've done. So we'll turn our attention now to what it takes to ensure that you do get paid.

### THE MECHANICS OF BILLING YOUR CLIENTS

- Handle billing in an orderly, regular, professional manner.

- Log the time and expenses that you put in when working for each client as soon as possible after you complete a task. Your records will be much more accurate if you don't let hours or expenses accumulate for days or weeks before logging them.

- Make accuracy a priority. Nothing irritates clients more than being billed for time or expense items they didn't receive.

- Use software to generate a professional looking invoice.

- Before you start work, find out who in the company is supposed to get your invoices. Make sure you spell their name correctly and have their proper title on both your envelope and the invoice.

- Mail invoices on a regular schedule. If you don't bill regularly, don't expect clients to pay regularly.

- Make sure that you log in all payments immediately. Billing twice for work the client has already paid for is sure to generate bad will.

### WHAT GOES ON AN INVOICE

1. A phone number to be called in case of a problem with the bill.

2. The client's company name, project name, and any client-supplied identifier(s) needed by their accounting system.

3. Your name and the names of any subcontractors or employees whose work is being billed for, your company address, and phone number.

4. For An Hourly Rate Project:

    - Hours spent during period, broken down by project, project phase, department or any other way that the client prefers.

    - The hourly rate at which the hours are billed

5. For A Fixed Rate Project:
   - Date of any contract-specified milestones that have passed.
   - The amount due at the milestone.
   - The total amount due.
6. The date by which payment is due and any discounts for early payment.
7. Itemized extraordinary expenses.

## TIME AND BILLING SOFTWARE

To help you manage and generate your invoices, you may want to use a time and billing software package designed especially for computer consultants. This kind of software is highly recommended especially if you work for more than a small number of clients a year.

A good time and billing package should be able to:

- Track several projects per client.
- Track billed and unbilled expenses and generate expense reports for you.
- Handle fixed rate projects.
- Track mileage, both billed and unbilled.
- Track sales tax for hardware and software sales.
- Track unused hours for retainer clients.
- Generate customized invoices.
- Generate useful reports.
- Create mailing labels for clients.
- Import and export data to other software.

## TIME AND BILLING SOFTWARE RECOMMENDATIONS

Popular Time and Billing Packages recommended by consultants include:

Time is Money  (Shareware—Martin Schiff)

Timeslips/Timeslips for Windows  (Timeslips)

Responsive Time Logger for Windows  (Shareware—Responsive Software)

## Example 12.  Sample Invoice Generated by "Time Is Money"

```
                        Computer Helper
                      473 Firestone Blvd.
                       Elgin, MA  01098
                     Phone:  413 471-0231



May 2, 1996                              INVOICE # CH10050



Elbert Dimsworthy, President
National Bait Inc.
1434 Snapper Road
Bayswater, MA  01083

                 INVOICE FOR CONSULTING SERVICES
=================================
Project:  Fleet Management System


   DESCRIPTION OF ACTIVITY                    TIME     DATE
   ----------------------------------------------------------
   Install V. 2.1                              4   04/14/96


   Tune Windows                                1   04/14/96


   Install Microsoft Office                    1   04/15/96
   ----------------------------------------------------------
   TOTAL .......6 Hrs @  $50 per hour         $    300



   EXPENSES OR MISCELLANEOUS CHARGES                  AMOUNT
   ----------------------------------------------------------


   Microsoft Office Upgrade                        $  249.95


==============================================================
   TOTAL AMOUNT DUE ................................. $  549.95

INVOICE DUE ON RECEIPT.  THANK YOU VERY MUCH!
```

## WATCH OUT FOR PAYMENT PROBLEMS

One very big difference between being a consultant and being an employee is that when you are working on an assignment as a consultant, you can never assume you are going to get paid.

Sadly, what you can assume is that many clients will withhold payment until the last possible moment—including, and indeed, especially, huge multinational firms.

You will have to keep a close eye on your unpaid invoices and take action when a respectable amount of time has gone by without payment to make sure that what you are dealing with is *slow* payment, rather than *no* payment. A vigilant approach to monitoring collections can keep any losses low if it does turn out that you are dealing with a deadbeat client. To avoid serious damage to your business you should feel justified in refusing to let *any* client run up a significant tab.

Look at the following list of real life situations for hints on how to ensure that you do get paid—eventually.

### *SOLVING COMMON PAYMENT PROBLEMS*

***PROBLEM:*** The client has agreed to pay you a down payment or other form of advance before you begin work but you haven't received it by the time work is scheduled to begin.

***PROPER RESPONSE:*** Do *not* start work without the advance in hand. If the client can't come up with this payment, what makes you think they will come up with the rest of your pay? Politely explain that you'll be happy to start work as soon as you get the agreed upon advance and don't give into cajolery.

***PROBLEM:*** The client, a Fortune 500 company, is four months behind on paying your invoices.

***PROPER RESPONSE:*** Many large corporations are notorious slow to pay. If you've done your credit check—as you should have done before taking on any new client—and if the company is one that is known to pay its bills—eventually—ask your contact at the company to check on the status of your invoice, or else contact the accounting department on your own to see if you can expedite matters. However, you may just have to wait until the company decides to pay you. This corporate slowness to pay is one reason some consultants work through third party consulting firms who will pay them without regard to when the client pays.

**PROBLEM:** You have sent the client, a local midsize manufacturer, three invoices each covering two weeks of work. You have yet to receive a dime.

**PROPER RESPONSE:** Notify the client that there seems to be a problem with your invoices and ask what you need to do to resolve it. If the client can't come up with a justifiable reason for the payment delay, insist and that you have a firm policy of not continuing to work for a client when more than two current invoices are unpaid. If the invoices stay unpaid, politely inform the client that you will return to complete the work when you receive payment for the open invoices. If you hesitate to do this because you worry about alienating a client, ask yourself what kind of client is alienated when you ask for payment on a bill that is past 45 days due?

**PROBLEM:** You sent your invoices and received payment. Unfortunately, it was for an amount much smaller than what you billed.

**PROPER RESPONSE:** Immediately contact the client and ask them politely to explain the reason behind the discrepancy. If it isn't a simple error—which it may be—clear up whatever the problem is before doing more work. If the client is unhappy with your work or says you haven't done something you have billed for, make sure there isn't a basis for this complaint. If there is, ask the client what you need to do to resolve the problem. If there is no basis, or if the problem cannot be resolved and the client refuses to pay, you may have to suggest that the client replace you with another consultant. Do *not* continue working in a way that suggests that you have accepted the half-payments as payment for your previous services.

**PROBLEM:** After you work on a project for a while, the client announces that he's going to have to pay less than you'd agreed to for the rest of the project.

**PROPER RESPONSE:** If the client claims hardship as the reason for this request, it's up to you how you want to handle it. But be sure a real hardship exists, so that you don't end up working at a much lower rate and then read in your local paper about the client's record earnings. Some larger corporations may try to impose to impose a unilateral rate-drop on consultants as part of a fanatical cost-cutting strategy. If this happens to you, don't be afraid to let the client know you won't take that kind of treatment and that you are prepared to walk away from the contract if the client insists on breaching it.

**PROBLEM:** The client's final payment for the custom software you developed for him is four months overdue.

**PROPER RESPONSE:** Explain that you will not be able to answer any further calls for support for the system until payment is made. Unfortunately, failure to pay the final payment is very common, since by then you've lost most of your leverage over the client. So try to keep these final payments small.

**PROBLEM:** When you inquire about an overdue invoice, you are told "We're just about to put the check in the mail."

**PROPER RESPONSE:** Tell them that you'll be right over to pick it up, and do—or send a messenger.

**PROBLEM:** Your contract requires you to buy and install expensive computers on the client's site. You have asked for a down payment on the equipment, but you have not received it.

**PROPER RESPONSE:** Do not deliver the hardware until you get your down payment if it was in your contract that one was be paid. Once the client takes possession of hardware or software, you will not be able to repossess it unless you have a time-payment contract with the client—even if the client doesn't pay. Failure to pay the down payment does not bode well for the likelihood of your receiving any further payment.

**PROBLEM:** You are working on another client request when the client's hard drive crashes. The client asks you to buy a new hard drive and install it for him.

**PROPER RESPONSE:** Write an addendum to the original contract describing the service the client has asked you to perform and specifying the cost of the hard drive. Have the client sign it before you buy or install anything. You may also ask for a deposit on the cost of the hard drive. Otherwise, you may end up having difficulty getting paid for the service—especially if the client convinces himself, later, that you "broke" the drive.

**PROBLEM:** The consulting company you are working for pays you with an out-of-state check that bounces when you deposit it. When you call up you are told it's a "bookkeeping error." The second check, delivered a few days later clears.

**PROPER RESPONSE:** This happens more often than you'd expect. Sometimes it is indeed a simple error, but there are a few large consulting companies with offices around the U.S. and abroad who are notorious for bouncing their checks. Because they're also notorious for some other unethical practices, if you experience more than one or at most two such problems with payment from a consulting company of any size take it as a warning and start hunting—quickly—for another consulting company to work for.

## GOTCHA!!

If a client goes bankrupt or just plain does not have the money to pay your invoices, you may never see a dime of your money, no matter what wording you included on your contract or the strength of your legal case.

That's why you must make it a policy to never let any unpaid invoice get large enough that if a client defaults it could put you out of business.

## HOW TO HANDLE NONPAYMENT

When payment on outstanding invoices lags way beyond an acceptable time period, take the following steps:

1. Contact the client and inquire whether there is a problem with any item that appears on the bill.

2. Call the person in the accounting department who has responsibility for getting the bills out and ask them to explain why you haven't yet received payment.

3. If they tell you the check is "about to go in the mail" offer to pick it up in person that afternoon.

4. Refuse to do any further work or to answer any support calls until payment is made. Ideally, you should have specified that you would do this in the contract's "Method of Payment" clause.

5. Have your lawyer send an "Attorney Letter" on his stationary requesting payment and suggesting that you will take legal action if it isn't forthcoming.

6. Call the clerk of the local Small Claims court and inquire what the limit is for small claims in your state. (Expect it to be somewhere from $1,000 to $5,000.) If your claim is under this amount, you can go through small claims court to get a judgment without a lawyer being required. You may NOT, however, split a larger invoice into a series of small claims.

7. Contact a reputable collection agency and turn the problem over to them for a percentage of the take. It will cost you some money, but it is a lot cheaper than suing and you don't pay unless the agency collects.

## MAINTAINING THE CLIENT RELATIONSHIP AFTER THE JOB IS OVER

Once you've finished the job your challenge is to encourage the client to keep in touch with you, at the same time as you discourage the client from wasting your time with calls for help with frivolous problems.

Doing this often requires that you walk a tightrope. You must set boundaries to avoid having clients call you every time they feel too lazy to refer to a manual, but you don't want to give them the feeling you don't care about their problems, since you do want them to bring you in on future projects.

Here are some guidelines that will help you turn support into a profit center while maintaining a positive relationship with your clients:

## TURN SUPPORT INTO A PROFIT CENTER

### ENSURE THAT SUPPORT IS BILLABLE BY:

- Educating the client as to the difference between fixes and support.
- Having clearly defined acceptance testing and sign-off criteria.
- Providing free support for a limited time after sign-off but making the limits of this free support clear and billing for any work that is *not in* support of the original project.
- Responding to requests for support on a sliding scale: quickly right after the project is complete, and then with a longer interval as project ages.
- Educating the client about the difference between support and training.
- Billing for nuisance calls from people who want endless support but clearly have no intention of buying further services.

### ENSURE THAT CLIENTS COME BACK TO YOU BY:

- Distinguishing between "on the clock" calls and calls to keep the relationship alive. Don't bill clients for friendly chit-chat.
- Giving existing clients priority over new ones.
- Offering discounted rates for a set number of prepaid support hours with a further discount for hours over the set number.
- Selling 800 phone service (or unlimited phone support) for a fixed annual rate.

## GOTCHA!!

### SUPPORT RESPONSE TIME

Unless you have a lot of experience with writing—and living up to—service level agreements, be extremely careful with any wording you include in support contracts that obliges you to respond to a client's problem within a specific time frame.

- Be realistic when setting the response time you commit to.

- Distinguish between "response"—contacting the client and "resolution"—making the problem go away.

- Make sure that the wording you agree to on any support contract does not penalize you for unavoidable delays.

## CONCLUSION

With this, we've completed our survey of what you need to know to get started in computer consulting. The material you've found here is the kind of information you can learn from a book intended for a broad audience. To go beyond it you'll need to find experienced consultants in your own niche who can give you specific information about the unique requirements of that niche and its clientele.

An experienced mentor can help you overcome the challenges that lie in wait for you. But to attract that kind of mentor you'll have to do the best you can with the resources you have now. Hone your technical and business skills, do the best job possible for your clients, and do what you can to help other consultants you may meet. By doing all this, you will become someone that people worth having as mentors will *want* to help.

So here's wishing you joy and the best of luck in your consulting career!

# Appendix A

# BUSINESS COMMUNICATIONS BASICS

## HOW TO WRITE AN EFFECTIVE BUSINESS LETTER

### *FORMAT*

✎ Use Pica (12 point) type. Courier is always a good choice for a letter as it makes your letter look like a letter. Use a smaller font if it will keep your letter all on one page. Whatever font you choose, make sure it's easy to read.

✎ Put the date at the top, skip a few lines and block the recipient's address along the left column. Make sure you spell the recipient's name, business name, and job title correctly. If you have any question about them, call the company switchboard and ask the receptionist for the spellings and job title.

✎ If your letter is about a specific invoice, policy number, or other such item, put in a "RE:" line after the recipient's address. (Example: "RE Invoice 432145, Dated 7/24/1995.) Otherwise do *not* put in a subject line.

✎ Break your letter into three paragraphs and center the letter vertically on the page.

✎ Sign off business correspondence with "Yours truly" or "Sincerely."

✎ Always include your telephone number in the text of the letter if you want the recipient to call you, even if it is on your letterhead. If you are only available at certain set times, include a line saying when you can be reached.

✎ Put your email address on your letter if you are replying to someone you met on-line.

✎ Spellcheck everything in the letter and spellcheck it again if you make changes.

## CONTENT

✐ Have a specific goal in mind when you write a letter and limit yourself to getting across no more than three important points. Don't try to do too much in a single letter.

✐ Remember that busy people rarely read anything carefully, and that your recipient may not give your letter a full reading, and make your main points as clearly as possible.

✐ Never try to make a sale in a letter. Use letters to convey interesting information, but do any selling face-to-face or on the phone.

✐ If you are writing the letter to reinforce points discussed in a previous phone conversation or interview, begin your letter with a phrase like, "I greatly enjoyed the phone conversation we had on Thursday. As we discussed then... ."

✐ End all letters by indicating briefly the response you hope to receive. Some examples of good closings are:"I look forward to hearing from you after you've had a chance to review the enclosed material." or, "Call me at 486-8147 at any time if you'd like to discuss this further." or, "If I don't hear anything further from you by next week, I'll fax you a copy of the contract as it is described here."

✐ The standard ending for a business letter is, "If you require any further information please do not hesitate to contact me." But only use this if you aren't looking for an actual reply. If you are, describe the reply you would like to receive.

✐ Avoid using a mass mailing format and advertising phraseology like "Once-in-a-lifetime opportunity," "Free!" "For a limited time only!" "Don't ignore this amazing offer" or "Act now!"

# HOW TO MAKE THE BEST USE OF THE PHONE

☎ Before you make an important business phone call, jot down on a piece of paper the main point you'll make in your introductory phrase. Then list any other pieces of essential information you wish to convey to or find out from the person you are calling.

☎ Keep your phone agenda tight and focused on a few main points. Don't attempt to do too much in one call.

☎ Ask "is this a good time to talk" before launching into a long discussion. If the answer is, "No," ask when *would* be a good time to call and call back then. Try to arrange it so that you promise to call back yourself rather than agreeing to wait for the caller to call you back.

☎ Remember to turn off call waiting before you call an important client. (And remember to turn it back on when you're done!)

☎ Consider using email to initiate a first contact, both to avoid telephone screening systems and to introduce yourself in a way that allows you to include more substantial information.

☎ If you get voicemail when cold calling, it is best to call back rather than leave a message. However, if you keep reaching voicemail, you may have no alternative except to leave a message.

## *HOW TO GET PAST VOICEMAIL*

☎ Do *not* deliver a sales pitch onto the voicemail system.

☎ Always indicate in your message whom you are trying to reach.

☎ Speak slowly and pronounce your name carefully. If you leave a long message, repeat your telephone number at the end of the message.

☎ If you are forced to leave an important message on voicemail be sure you include the name of the person you are calling and your telephone number in case phones have been reassigned or you have reached a wrong number.

☎ If you must leave a message on a voicemail system or answering machine, keep a card containing your written list of important points near the phone so you can quickly orient yourself when you get called back.

The most effective message to leave on a voicemail system when cold calling is either your name alone, for example, "This is Joe Blodgett calling Ed Snippett. Please call me at 123-4567" Or use your name and a brief identifier, for example, "This is Joe Blodgett, of Blodgett Computer Services calling Ed Snippet to discuss Network Support services." Keep your notes handy so you can respond properly when people respond to your voicemail. The examples below show the importance of delivering a prepared response.

### Example 13. Unprepared Response

| | |
|---|---|
| ***Brrrring!*** | |
| **You:** | *Blodgett Computer Services, Joe Blodgett speaking.* |
| **Caller:** | *This is Ed <mumble>. I'm returning your call.* |
| **You:** | *What was that name again?* |
| **Caller:** | *<Slightly annoyed> Ed Mumble.* |
| **You:** | *And what company did you say you were with.* |
| **Caller:** | *<Testily> Megacorp.* |
| **You:** | *Let's see, you're the manager of printing services at Megacorp?* |
| **Caller:** | *No. I'm the vice president of MIS.* |
| **You:** | *Oh, that's right. <sheepishly> Well, let's see now. What did I call you about? Oh yes, I wanted to discuss our network support services with you.* |
| **Caller:** | *Sorry, we're not interested. <hangs up>* |

### Example 14. Prepared Response

| | |
|---|---|
| ***Brrrring!*** | |
| **You:** | *Blodgett Computer Services, Joe Blodgett speaking.* |
| **Caller:** | *This is Ed <mumble> returning your call.* |
| **You:** | *Ed, great to hear from you! I'm calling because I think you may be interested in hearing about a new support service we're offering. It lets us provide timely, cost-effective network support to companies like Megacorp that need 100% reliability for their networks. Are you satisfied with the service you're getting now for the networks you rely on?* |
| **Caller:** | *Well, as a matter of fact, we have been discussing improving our network support . . ..* |

# Appendix B

# ICCA STANDARD FORM CONTRACT

The following contract was designed by the Independent Computer Consultants Association as a model for the use of its membership. Do not use it in your own business without first having it reviewed by an attorney who specializes in computer or intellectual property law as it may need to be adapted to conform to the specific legal requirment in effect in your state.

INDEPENDENT COMPUTER CONSULTANTS ASSOCIATION

STANDARD FORM CONSULTING CONTRACT

THIS AGREEMENT is made as of_____, 19 _____,

between _____("Client")

and _____ ("Consultant").

In the event of a conflict in the provisions of any attachments hereto and the provisions set forth in this Agreement, the provisions of such attachments shall govern.

1. **Services.** Consultant agrees to perform for Client the services listed in the Scope of Services section in Exhibit A, attached hereto and executed by both Client and Consultant. Such services are hereinafter referred to as "Services". Client agrees that consultant shall have ready access to Client's staff and resources as necessary to perform the Consultant's services provided for by this contract.

2. **Rate of Payment for Services.** Client agrees to pay Consultant for Services in accordance with the schedule contained in Exhibit B attached hereto and executed by both Client and Consultant.

3. **Invoicing.** Client shall pay the amounts agreed to herein upon receipt of invoices which shall be sent by Consultant, and Client shall pay the amount of such invoices to Consultant.

4. **Confidential Information.** Each party hereto ("Such Party") shall hold in trust for the other party hereto ("Such Other Party"), and shall not disclose to any non-party to the Agreement, any confidential information of such Other Party. Confidential information is information which relates to Such Other Party's research, development, trade secrets or business affairs, but does not include information which is generally known or easily ascertainable by non-parties of ordinary skill in computer systems design and programming.

Consultant hereby acknowledges that during the performance of this contract, the Consultant may learn or receive confidential Client information and therefore Consultant hereby confirms that all such information relating to the client's business will be kept confidential by the Consultant, except to the extent that such information is required to be divulged to the Consultant's clerical or support staff or associates in order to enable Consultant to perform Consultant's contract obligation.

5. **Staff.** Consultant is an independent contractor and neither Consultant nor Consultant's staff is or shall be deemed to be employed by Client. Client is hereby contracting with Consultant for the services described on Exhibit A and Consultant reserves the right to determine the method, manner and mean by which the services will be performed. Consultant is not required to perform the services during a fixed hourly or daily time and if the services are performed at the Client's premises, then Consultants time spent at the premises is to be at the discretion of the Consultant; subject to the Client's normal business hours and security requirements. Consultant hereby confirms to Client that Client will not be required to furnish or provide any training to Consultant to enable Consultant to perform services required hereunder. The services shall be performed by Consultant or Consultant's staff, and Client shall not be required to hire, supervise or pay any assistants to help Consultant who performs the services under this agreement. Consultant shall not be required to devote Consultant's full time nor the full time of Consultant's staff to the performance of the services required hereunder, and it is acknowledged that Consultant has other Clients and Consultant offers services to the general public. The order or sequence in which the work is to be performed shall be under the control of Consultant. Except to the extent that the Consultant's work must be performed on or with Client's computers or Client's existing software, all materials used in providing the services shall be provided by Consultant. Consultant's services hereunder cannot be terminated or cancelled short of completion of the services agreed upon except for Consultant's failure to perform the contract's specification as required hereunder and conversely, subject to Client's obligation to make full and timely payment(s) for Consultant's services as set forth in Exhibit B, Consultant shall be obligated to complete the services agreed upon and shall be liable for non-performance of the services to the extent and as provided in Paragraph 10 hereof. Client shall not provide any insurance coverage of any kind for Consultant or Consultant's staff, and Client will not withhold any amount that would normally be withheld from an employee's pay. Consultant shall take appropriate measures to insure that Consultant's staff is competent and that they do not breach Section 4 hereof.

Each of the parties hereto agrees that, while performing Services under this Agreement, and for a period of six (6) months following the termination of this Agreement, neither party will, except with the other party's written approval, solicit or offer employment to the other party's employees or staff engaged in any efforts under this Agreement.

6. **Use of Work Product.** Except as specifically set forth in writing and signed by both Client and Consultant, Consultant shall have all copyright and patent rights with respect to all materials developed under this contract, and Client is hereby granted a non-exclusive license to use and employ such materials within the Client's business.

7. **Client Representative.** The following individual _____ shall represent the Client during the performance of this contract with respect to the services and deliverables as defined herein and has authority to execute written modifications or additions to this contract as defined in Section 14.

8. **Disputes.** Any disputes that arise between the parties with respect to the performance of this contract shall be submitted to binding arbitration by the American Arbitration Association, to be determined and resolved by said Association under its rules and procedures in effect at the time of submission and the parties hereby agree to share equally in the costs of said arbitration.

The final arbitration decision shall be enforceable through the courts of the state of Consultant's address [15(ii)] or any other state in which the Client resides or may be located. In the event that this arbitration provision is held unenforceable by any court of competent jurisdiction, then this contract shall be as binding and enforceable as if this section 8 were not a part hereof.

9. **Taxes.** Any and all taxes, except income taxes, imposed or assessed by reason of this contract or its performance, including but not limited to sales or use taxes, shall be paid by the Client. Consultants shall be responsible for any taxes or penalties assessed by reason of any claims that Consultant is an employee of Client and Client and Consultant specifically agree that Consultant is not an employee of Client.

## LIMITED WARRANTY

10. **Liability.** Consultant warrants to Client that the material, analysis, data, programs and services to be delivered or rendered hereunder, will be of the kind and quality designated and will be performed by qualified personnel. Special requirements for format or standards to be followed shall be attached as an additional Exhibit and executed by both Client and Consultant. **Consultant makes no other warranties, whether written, oral or implied, including without limitation, warranty of fitness for purpose or merchantability.** In no event shall Consultant be liable for special or consequential damages, either in contract or tort, whether or not the possibility of such damages has been disclosed to Consultant in advance or could have been reasonably foreseen by Consultant, and in the event this limitation of damages is held unenforceable then the parties agree that by reason of the difficulty in foreseeing possible damages all liability to Client shall be limited to One Hundred Dollars ($100.00) as liquidated damages and not as a penalty.

11. **Complete Agreement.** This agreement contains the entire agreement between the parties hereto with respect to the matters covered herein. No other agreements, representations, warranties or other matters, oral or written, purportedly agreed to or represented by or on behalf of Consultant by any of its employees or agents, or contained in any sales materials or brochures, shall be deemed to bind the parties hereto with respect to the subject matter hereof. Client acknowledges that it is entering into this Agreement solely on the basis of the representations contained herein.

12. **Applicable Law.** Consultant shall comply with all applicable laws in performing Services but shall be held harmless for violation of any governmental procurement regulation to which it may be subject but to which reference is not made in Exhibit A. This Agreement shall be construed in accordance with the laws of the State indicated by the Consultant's address [15 (ii)].

13. **Scope of Agreement.** If the scope of any of the provisions of the Agreement is too broad in any respect whatsoever to permit enforcement to its full extent, then such provisions shall be enforced to the maximum extent permitted by law, and the parties hereto consent and agree that such scope may be judicially modified accordingly and that the whole of such provisions of this Agreement shall not thereby fail, but that the scope of such provisions shall be curtailed only to the extent necessary to conform to law.

14. **Additional Work.** After receipt of an order which adds to the Services, Consultant may, at its discretion, take reasonable action and expend reasonable amounts of time and money based on such order. Client agrees to pay Consultant for such action and expenditure as set forth in Exhibit B of this Agreement for payments related to Services.

15. **Notices.**
(i) Notices to Client should be sent to:

(ii) Notices to Consultant should be sent to:

16. **Assignment.** This Agreement may not be assigned by either party without the prior written consent of the other party. Except for the prohibition on assignment contained in the preceding sentence, this Agreement shall be binding upon and inure to the benefits of the heirs, successors and assigns of the parties hereto.

IN WITNESS WHEREOF, the parties hereto have signed this Agreement as of the date first above written. **THIS CONTRACT CONTAINS A BINDING ARBITRATION PROVISION WHICH MAY BE ENFORCED BY THE PARTIES.**

| | |
|---|---|
| Client | Consultant |

Type Name and Title

(This is a Standard Form Contract which may or may not require revision by the individual consultant's legal counsel. It is recommended that each consultant review the legal requirements pertaining to the consultant's State of operation with counsel licensed to practice in that State. Various States have laws that require that disclaimers of liability or arbitration provisions must be printed in enlarged print or that specific language be used, which may or may not be contained in this form. This should be reviewed with the counsel in the State in which each Consultant operates.)

For use by ICCA Members only. Copyright, October, 1993.
**Independent Computer Consultants Association** 933 Gardenview Office Pkwy. St. Louis, MO 63141, FAX 314-567-5133; Phone 314-997-4633

Copyright ICCA. Used by Permission

# INDEX

## We Want To Hear From You!

If you have comments on this book or information you'd like to share with other consultants, please drop us a line here at:

**Technion Books**

**P.O. Box 171**

**Leverett, MA  01054**

# Other Products You Can Order from Technion Books:

### THE COMPUTER CONSULTANT'S STARTER SET  $25

Available in November, 1995, this set includes:

- A sample copy of *The Computer Consultant's Update*, Janet Ruhl's newsletter.

- **PC Shareware** for consultants including  DOS Time and Billing software.

- A **Resource Guide** listing books, magazines, organizations, and vendor programs of interest to computer consultants.

- An updated **Rate Survey**.

- A free **Compuserve Sign-on Package** (total value $25) which gives you Compuserve software, a one-month subscription to Compuserve, and $15 dollars of free connect time. Come visit the Computer Consultants Forum!

### THE COMPUTER CONSULTANT'S UPDATE  $30

Too busy to read all the messages on Compuserve's Computer Consultants Forum? Now you can keep abreast of new marketing ideas, ways of getting paid, strategies for dealing with client problems, and legal and accounting changes with Janet Ruhl's new newsletter. This introductory subscription gives you three issues.